T0328797

Cambridge Elements ☰

Elements in Ancient Philosophy
edited by
James Warren
University of Cambridge

PROPERTIES
IN ANCIENT METAPHYSICS

Anna Marmodoro
Durham University

CAMBRIDGE
UNIVERSITY PRESS

Shaftesbury Road, Cambridge CB2 8EA, United Kingdom

One Liberty Plaza, 20th Floor, New York, NY 10006, USA

477 Williamstown Road, Port Melbourne, VIC 3207, Australia

314–321, 3rd Floor, Plot 3, Splendor Forum, Jasola District Centre,
New Delhi – 110025, India

103 Penang Road, #05–06/07, Visioncrest Commercial, Singapore 238467

Cambridge University Press is part of Cambridge University Press & Assessment,
a department of the University of Cambridge.

We share the University's mission to contribute to society through the pursuit of
education, learning and research at the highest international levels of excellence.

www.cambridge.org
Information on this title: www.cambridge.org/9781009475730

DOI: 10.1017/9781009105866

First published 2023

A catalogue record for this publication is available from the British Library

ISBN 978-1-009-47573-0 Hardback
ISBN 978-1-009-10146-2 Paperback
ISSN 2631-4118 (online)
ISSN 2631-410X (print)

Properties in Ancient Metaphysics

Elements in Ancient Philosophy

DOI: 10.1017/9781009105866
First published online: November 2023

Anna Marmodoro
Durham University

Author for correspondence: Anna Marmodoro,
anna.marmodoro@durham.ac.uk

Abstract: This Element provides an overview of how the ancient thinkers (Anaxagoras, Plato and Aristotle) theorised about properties; such overview puts in relief the inquiries, problems and solutions they were pursuing while engaged in dialogue with each other. It examines alternative philosophical perspectives existing in antiquity concerning the explanation of property qualification, qualitative similarity, compositeness, and oneness. It further argues that although Plato was the first to conceptualise recurring universals, he did not reify them and did not admit them in his ontology; it was Aristotle who did, and developed his metaphysics around them. Aristotle, building on Plato's work, identified the metaphysical phenomenon of the instantiation of properties and developed an account for it. Finally, this Element outlines Aristotle's 'sophisticated' account of the oneness of a substance and argues that it was not hylomorphic.

Keywords: Anaxagoras, Plato, Aristotle, properties, resemblance

ISBNs: 9781009475730 (HB), 9781009101462 (PB), 9781009105866 (OC)
ISSNs: 2631-4118 (online), 2631-410X (print)

Contents

1 Introduction

1.1 Aims and Argument

This Element provides an overview of how some of the most philosophically influential thinkers of classical antiquity theorised about properties. It puts in relief the inquiries, problems and solutions the ancients were pursuing while engaged in dialogue with each other, within their philosophical *milieu*. Furthermore, it aims to make their different theories of properties known and accessible to today's philosophers, thus tracking the genealogy of some of our current metaphysical positions and debates on the topic.

We will examine whether the ancient Greek philosophers under consideration thought of properties as particulars or universals; and, furthermore, how they conceived of and accounted metaphysically for the occurence of properties in the world and their instantiation in objects, the qualification of objects by properties, the resemblance between objects with respect to their properties, and the oneness of complexes of properties as individual objects – an important and difficult question for ancient and modern philosophers alike.

Some of the interpretations put forward here will surprise the reader, because they throw off centre an entrenched scholarly approach concerning how the ancients thought about properties. It is a philosophical commonplace to identify Plato and Aristotle as the two main players in the ancient debate on properties, and to interpret both of them as positing universals, which are transcendent for the one and immanent for the other; that is, for Plato, existing independently from the concrete particular objects in the world (*ante res*), and for Aristotle, existing as dependent on such objects (*in rebus*). Here I will show that the two main players who shaped our modern metaphysics of properties, and ought to be given the central stage, are instead Anaxagoras, on the one hand (for whom properties are particular), and Aristotle, on the other (for whom properties are universal), with Plato innovating, experimenting and vacillating 'in-between', as it were, the positions of his predecessor and his successor.[1]

We need, I contend, to delve into Anaxagoras's, Plato's and Aristotle's views and study them comparatively (as it is rarely done; Mann (2000) is a notable exception) to understand them fully; their respective theories of properties were

---

[1] The reader might want to ask why these three and not other ancient Greek thinkers are included here. This Element does not aim to cover in full all that the ancients thought about properties, but rather to reconstruct the *fil rouge* that runs through the main theories of properties in antiquity which have shaped the development of today's metaphysics of properties, and for this Anaxagoras, Plato and Aristotle are the three key figures.

developed by each trying to solve philosophical problems that were left open by
their precedecessors, or taking forward solutions left undeveloped.[2]

1.2 Qualification and Similarity

A common way at least in modern philosophy to introduce the question of what
properties are is *via* the problem of qualitative similarity. There are innumérable
instances of qualitative similarity in the world: my table and my chair are each
and both brown; we are all human beings; these two triangles have the same
shape; and so on. Philosophers treat qualitative similarity as a given fact;
D. M. Armstrong calls it a 'Moorean fact': '[T]he fact of sameness of type is
a Moorean fact: one of the many facts which even philosophers should not deny,
whatever philosophical account or analysis they give of such facts. Any com-
prehensive philosophy must try to give some account of Moorean facts. They
constitute the compulsory questions in the [= any] philosophical examination
paper' (1980: 442).

A. S. Maurin explicates Armstrong's words, and the significance for philosophers of acknowledging something as a Moorean fact, thus: 'Facts that we on
pain of irrationality understand, cannot doubt, and must accept as true – in other
words, Moorean facts – are facts that must be given what Moore calls 'an
analysis' and what later philosophers have called 'an account' or 'an explanation'. And what accounts for or (metaphysically) explains these facts is neither
trivial nor incontrovertible' (2022:7).

Suppose that we all agree that qualitative similarity is a Moorean fact, and we
try to explain it. What conceptual tools do we need to provide such an explanation? Let us start by asking ourselves this (challenging) question: can we
conceptualise two objects that are qualitatively similar to one another (e.g. they
are both round), but share nothing in common in their respective constitutions? If
we cannot, that is if we need to posit that they share something in common in their
respective constitutions, what will this be, and how will it feature in our ontology?
Alternatively, we can treat qualitative similarity as a brute fact, with no additional
item in the ontology underpinning it; but appealing to brute facts is never an
uncontroversial choice, and rarely a favourite one among philosophers.

D. M. Armstrong and D. Lewis are modern representatives of opposing ways
of answering the question of what accounts for qualitive similarity. They agree
the question demands an answer; but Lewis argues that

---

[2] This Element includes material drawn from other publications of mine, as indicated case by case;
    that material is here embedded in a new overall argument and in most cases developed further/in
    new directions with respect to the previously published version.

[t]here are three ways to give an account. (1) 'I deny it [i.e. qualitative similarity]' – this earns a failing mark [in the proverbial philosophical examination paper mentioned by Armstrong] if the fact is really Moorean. (2) 'I analyse it thus' – this is Armstrong's response to the facts of apparent sameness of type. Or (3) 'I accept it as primitive'. Not every account is an analysis! A system that takes certain Moorean facts as primitive and unanalyzed cannot be accused of failing to make a place for them. It neither shirks the compulsory question nor answers it by denial. It does give an account. (1983: 352)

Armstrong doesn't think so: for him, saying 'It's ultimate' or 'It's primitive' or 'It's brute' doesn't count as giving an account or explanation. If qualitative similarity is to be explained, something has to be added to the ontology that resembling objects share.

Enter properties! As Maurin notes, 'That properties can fill this [explanatory] need is accepted by most' today (2022: 6), and, I add, by the ancient Greeks, too. While the reader is encouraged to think of where they stand (and why) on this matter, the ancient Greek philosophers would have sided with Armstrong, both in thinking that qualitative similarity is (what we call) a Moorean fact, and in being unsatisfied with the idea that qualitative similarity is metaphysically primitive.[3]

In seeking an account of resemblance by way of this approach, the ancients – speaking broadly – proceed with an implicit acceptance of what has become known as the *Principle of Sufficient Reason*, namely that everything has a reason or a cause. An interesting, controversial and thought-provoking discussion of the principle and its ancient 'roots' is in Della Rocca (2020). In their theories of properties and property qualification, the ancients all aim to identify the *reason* that is *sufficient* to explain why something comes to be qualified in a certain way, and therefore also qualitatively similar to other things, by means of what I call the *Contagion Principle*. According to this principle, x becomes (or, is) f because y, which is already f, transmits (or, has transmitted) f-*ness* to x, which is (or was) not already f. This basic and, I contend, intuitive principle underpins the different models that individual ancient thinkers propose to account for property possession and similarity, as I will show in the sections to follow.

---

[3] Anaxagoras will ultimately not be able to do better than assume that qualification and similarity are brute facts in the case of his fundamental entities, the so-called Opposites; Plato, too, will have to posit that his Forms are primitively f, to block the *Third Man Argument*; and Aristotle does the same with his forms in his *Essence Regress*, as we will see in the relevant sections of this Element. The fact that these philosophers conclude their quest for explanation having accepted some primitives, does not however undermine the fact that they were genuinely engaged in seeking a primitives-free explanation.

Developing a suitable theory of property qualification that accounts for qualitative similarity became progressively one of greatest metaphysical challenges for the ancients. Here I will present how the challenge arose in Anaxagoras's account of the natural world; how much it troubled Plato; and how Aristotle made significant progress in addressing it. These three thinkers all addressed the question through pioneering ideas, which their successors have continued to explore to the present day.

1.3 The *One over Many Principle*

How do properties fulfil their explanatory role for qualitative similarity? It is generally assumed that they do so by what has become known as the *One over Many Principle*, that is: one and the same property is shared by many resembling objects. This principle is widely accepted in both ancient and modern metaphysics. Maurin reports a mainstream way of thinking of the issue:

> Many of those in favour of the existence of properties – including Plato, but see also (and perhaps especially) Armstrong (1978) – have then tied this problem to an argument: *the argument from the One over Many*. Here the idea has been that the sort of 'sameness' to which the fact of the One over Many […] draws our attention is most straightforwardly made sense of by literally accepting that there is one thing – the universal – that distinct objects share. (2022: 7, italics in the original)

Maurin adds an insightful observation, namely that 'one might get the impression that given this fact, (universal-)realism is inevitable. . . . Even if the fact of the One over Many – in appealing to 'sameness' and 'oneness' – on its surface seems especially suited to universal realism, that fact is better understood as neutral when it comes to which solution we ought to prefer'. (2022: 8)

I endorse the observation and I will show that, with respect to ancient metaphysics, the claim that qualitative similarity is explained through the *One over Many Principle* is misleading in its generality, because Anaxagoras, Plato and Aristotle have significantly different ways of implementing the principle. The issue of what is *One over Many* – that is, common among resembling objects – intersects with the issue of how the One is 'in' the Many.

1.4 How Is the One 'in' the Many?

If qualitative similarity among objects is explained by the presence of one and the same property 'in' the similar objects, how are properties 'in' the world? Two alternatives are in play in ancient metaphysics: the first is Anaxagoras's and the second Aristotle's. According to Anaxagoras, as we will see in Section 2, properties have their own spatial location; they don't depend on objects for it.[4] If however properties have a spatial location of their own, as particulars do, can properties be multiply located at once, so that one and the same property is in many objects? We will see that Anaxagoras addresses this problem by thinking of properties as mereologically distributed: a property (as a whole) is multilocated on account of its parts having different locations. Thus, resembling objects, for Anaxagoras, are such because they have within their respective constitutions parts of one and the same property.[5]

It is important to note here that difficulties emerge from Anaxagoras's account. First, the idea presupposed by this view, that properties have parts, is challenging and far from intuitive. *Ditto* for the idea that being qualified, for an object, is possessing parts of the property. We are familiar with the thought that material objects have parts, but Anaxagoras posits that properties have parts, and such parts are individuated independently of the objects the properties qualify. Second, the view that one and the same property is in many objects on account of the distribution of its parts among the objects raises the following problem: dividing up a property into parts, which are in objects somehow as functional 'proxies' of the property itself, appears to undermine the assumption that the property is one; for the property's parts serving as its proxies multiply the property, by qualifying the objects as if the property itself were in each of them. We will examine the metaphysical problems of attributing such a role and function to parts of properties, as well as investigate how each property part is individuated as that part. We will additionally consider whether postulating that one property is in the many by the distribution of its parts can serve as a sound solution to the problem of qualitative similarity. More generally, we will examine Anaxagoras's mereology of properties in Section 2 ; and its development, critical discussion and finally abandonment by Plato in Section 3.

Aristotle develops a very different metaphysics of properties from that of his predecessors, with an alternative account of qualification and qualitative similarity also, as we will see in Section 4. His most significant departure from Anaxagoras (and Plato) is to posit that properties are universals, which are 'in' the world as 'instantiated' in objects. The crux is how to understand what it is for a universal to be instantiated, and even multiply instantiated, that is: recurring whole in multiple locations at once. Explaining what being instantiated in

---

[4] Anaxagoras does not draw a sharp distinction in his system between properties and things (even if properties are more fundamental than things because properties make things up); Vlastos for example refers to Anaxagoras's properties with the expression 'substantial "quality-things"' (1950: 42).

[5] We will see in what follows that for Anaxagoras it is not the presence of a mere part of a property F that qualifies an object as a being *f*, but rather the presence of a preponderance of parts of the property F in the object that achieves this metaphysical result.

concrete particulars amounts to was a major challenge for Aristotle, and has continued to be a challenge for all philosophers who endorse a metaphysics of properties that is broadly Aristotelian. Aristotle's position, I contend, has not yet been studied adequately in the relevant literature, despite such literature being vast. According to the mainstream view, in the scholarly literature and also in ongoing discussions of Aristotle's theory in current metaphysics, instantiation is a single metaphysical phenomenon (while, I argue, there are *two* distinct ones that are confusedly referred to with the same term); and further, a universal is instantiated by combining hylomorphically with matter. This latter interpretation of Aristotle's position makes it generally unappealing and objectionable. On this account, many think that Aristotle's theory of recurrent universals and their instantiation in objects isn't philosophically sound. I will argue in Section 4 that it is sound, on a certain interpretation of Aristotle's key tenets.

The overall argument I will develop in this Element, across Sections 2, 3 and 4, is that there are two main positions in ancient metaphysics with respect to the explanation of qualification and of qualitative similarity among objects – I call them the *Distributive Model* and the *Recurrence Model* respectively. Anaxagoras and Plato (at least in most of his work, until his fresh start in the *Timaeus*) thought that properties are (respectively, physical or transcendent) particulars, which are distributed to the many objects in the world through their parts; for example, the pot is hot because it has part(s) of the property Hot in it. Aristotle thought instead that properties are abstract individual entities which recur in the many objects in the world; the pot is hot because the property Hot recurs whole in it (and in all other objects that are hot). I will argue here that only Aristotle's *Recurrence Model* successfully explains similarity. However, even if the *Distributive Model* is not able to deliver a philosophically sound account of qualitative similarity, both accounts were historically very influential, and for that time, tremendously innovative. Our history of the development of the metaphysics of properties, as we think of it today, would not be accurate or complete if we did not try to understand, not only where its pioneers succeeded, but also where they failed in charting what was then all new conceptual space.

Furthermore, on either the *Distributive* or the *Recurrence Model*, there is a problem that cannot be investigated in full in the present work, which I flag here for its importance for both the history of philosophy and for philosophy in general. Although Anaxagoras, Plato and Aristotle were adamant that it is not properties that change when 'in' the object (e.g. when a red rose changes in colour, it is not the redness in the rose that changes, but only the rose), Plato and especially Aristotle were aware that something happens to a property when it is 'in' an object and qualifies it. However, what it is that happens to the property still remains for us to conceptualise; neither we, nor the ancients have a term to refer to it. Let us say that when 'in' an object the property φs, using the verb 'to φ' as a placeholder. It is important that we endevour to understand what 'to φ' stands for; else we are pulled into theories of substance such as the Bundle Theory (whose difficulties are not within my remit to discuss here).

1.5 The Universality of Properties

The discussion of how One property is 'in' the Many, by distribution or by recurrence, sheds light on a related and much debated issue, namely whether the ancients conceived of properties as universals. While it is a commonplace, as already mentioned, to think that both Plato and Aristotle posited universal properties (only that for the former they are *ante res* and for the latter *in rebus*), this is not an accurate understanding of their positions. Plato explores alternative possibilities concerning this issue; but I argue that his position is that Forms are particular (Marmodoro 2021), while for example G. Fine (1993) and Harte (2008), among others, argue that they are universal, with many scholars simply assuming the latter view by default (e.g. Silverman, and Orilia & Paolini Paoletti in their respective *Stanford Encyclopedia of Philosophy* entries).[6] My view is that Plato's Forms are particulars, each of which is the unique *one* property type, which *many* similar objects have in common, and which explains their similarity; but each Form is also universal, in the specific sense that it is distributed in parts across the many similar objects (as Anaxagoras's Opposites are, particular and universal in the same way as Plato's Forms are, only that Anaxagoras's Opposites are physical, and not transcendent entities as Plato's property types are).

With respect to the status of Aristotle's forms, it is uncontroversial that they are universal, each recurring whole in multiple objects; but how to understand their universality is a debated issue. I will show that the way to understand the universality of Aristotle's forms is by abstraction from the objects they qualify; that is, if the chair and the table are brown, we can abstract the universal 'brownness' from each of the two objects in which it recurs, and thereby individuate it. This is how Aristotle conceives of the recurrence of properties: a property recurs because it can be abstracted from this or the other object.

---

[6] Silverman, Allan, 'Plato's Middle Period Metaphysics and Epistemology', *The Stanford Encyclopedia of Philosophy* (Fall 2022 Edition), Edward N. Zalta & Uri Nodelman (eds.), https://plato.stanford.edu/archives/fall2022/entries/plato-metaphysics/; Orilia, Francesco and Paolini Paoletti, Michele, 'Properties', *The Stanford Encyclopedia of Philosophy* (Spring 2022 Edition), Edward N. Zalta (ed.), https://plato.stanford.edu/archives/spr2022/entries/properties/.

1.6 Methodological Issues

This Element will introduce the reader to core ideas concerning the metaphysics of properties, studied from the complementary perspectives of scholars working on ancient philosophy as well as that of today's philosophers. The underlying methodological assumption is that we can understand what the ancients thought only from our own standpoint today.[7] To build conceptual bridges between them and us, for the sake of philosophical understanding, it is necessary to use modern terminology (such as 'qualification' or 'instantiation'). Even more importantly, it is necessary to acknowledge that there are (still) unexplored metaphysical insights to interpret in the ancient texts, as we will see in what follows, and much 'filling in' to be done to bring out what the ancients thought, but did not say in full.[8] This 'filling in' needs be done with due sensitivity to the historical and philosophical context in each case. But we need to recognise that we always 'fill in' when interpreting the ancients; so 'filling in' should become explicit and discussed as a philosophical contribution by the interpreter, aiming to show what the ancients thought or what would make their thought intelligible to us.

2 Anaxagoras's Opposites

Anaxagoras is an early Greek thinker whose significance is hard to overestimate in relation to the development of metaphysics, as we know it today. His ontology is built out of properties, the physical Opposites (such as the Hot, Cold, Wet, Dry, etc.), around which all Ionian cosmologies pivot at his time.[9] Anaxagoras, however, has his own original way of conceiving of the Opposites, as governed by mathematical and metaphysical principles that he pioneers. His principles are preserved to us in a handful of fragments, and yet, they have been at the centre of much controversy since antiquity and have had profound impact on Anaxagoras's philosophical successors, especially on Plato (as we will see in Section 3).

---

[7] I have articulated and defended with arguments this methodological approach in Marmodoro (2022b).

[8] I will illustrate, rather than define, what I mean 'filling in' by using some of my own interpretative work; for example, when Anaxagoras talks of the *preponderance of infinitesimals* in things, can we even conceptualise this thought, and if we can, what conception of infinity do we need to 'fill in'? Furthermore, I attribute an ontology of *qualitative gunk* to Anaxagoras; am I also thereby attributing *gunky spacetime* to him as well? Where does the 'attribution' end? These are examples of the type of interpretative issues I encountered in my work on Anaxagoras (in Marmodoro 2017).

[9] I capitalise Opposites when talking specifically about how Anaxagoras conceives of them, to indicate that his is not an ordinary conception.

2.1 Properties as Physical Particulars

In the extant fragments of Anaxagoras's work we find an indicative, even if not exhaustive, list of what properties there are in his world. According to fragment B4b, at a primordial stage in the history of the universe there exist the Opposites (e.g. the Wet and the Dry, the Hot and the Cold, the Bright and the Dark), stuffs (e.g. earth) and the so-called seeds.[10] All these items exist in a state of extreme mixture (a state that elsewhere, for example B1, B6, B11 and B12, Anaxagoras describes in terms of 'everything in everything'; to this we will return in Section 2.4). In B4b we read that,

> [b]efore there was separation off, because all things were together, there was not even any colour evident; for the mixture of all things prevented it, of the wet and the dry and of the hot and the cold and of the bright and the dark, and there was much earth present and seeds unlimited in number, in no way similar to one another. Since these things are so, it is right to think that all things were present in the whole.[11]

There is general agreement among scholars that Anaxagoras's Opposites (the Hot, the Cold, the Wet, the Dry, as representative examples) are metaphysically irreducible in his system; they don't derive from anything else more primitive than themselves. There is however more than the Opposites in Anaxagoras's world: as we just saw, earth is mentioned in B4b. Earth is not irreducible: in B15 we read that,

> [t]the dense and the wet and the cold and the dark come together here, where <the> earth is now; but the rare and the hot and the dry <and the bright> moved out to the far reaches of aether.

Taking earth as an example of stuff, and assuming that the same will apply *mutatis mutandis* to all kinds of stuffs, B15 indicates that while the Opposites are irreducible for Anaxagoras, stuffs (and hence objects made out of stuffs) are derivative from them.[12] How so? By aggregation and dissociation; we know from B4b (and from other fragments) that the Opposites can be moved spatially: they could be separated off from the primordial state of extreme mixture.

---

[10] I have discussed Anaxagoras's ontology and the fundamentality relations among what there is in it, in Marmodoro (2015, and 2017, Section 1.5). I don't reproduce here all my arguments.

[11] The quotations and translations of Anaxagoras's texts here provided, unless otherwise specified, are from Curd (2007).

[12] While there is general agreement on the fundamentality of the Opposites, scholars have taken different views on the issue of what else is fundamental in Anaxagoras's system. Curd (2007: 153ff) offers a helpful summary of the positions in the debate and of the arguments from all sides.

Nous, another fundamental entity in Anaxagoras's system, serves as the generator of spatial movement in the universe, by giving rise to a cosmic vortex that reshuffles 'things' (I use the term generically here); in B13 we read that

> [w]hen *Nous* began to move [things], there was separation off from the multitude that was being moved, and whatever *Nous* moved, all this was dissociated; and as things were being moved and dissociated, the revolution made them dissociate much more.

The shuffling around of the Opposites – their aggregation and separation – by means of a cosmic vortex started by *nous* gives rise to the ordinary objects of our experience, which furnish Anaxagoras's world at a successive, less primordial stage (as we know for example from B4a, which mentions the existence of human beings, other animals, plants, artefacts, households, cities and heavenly bodies).[13]

There is clear textual evidence that Anaxagoras thinks of the Opposites as subject to physical causation of different kinds. For instance, as we saw, they are impacted upon and set in movement by the cosmic vortex generated by *nous*, which can make them (or more precisely their parts) change spatial location. That the Opposites can be impacted upon by the vortex indicates that they are neither transcendent properties (like Plato's Forms) nor abstract properties (like Aristotle's forms). Anaxagoras's Opposites are physical particular properties; they exist in nature and are located in space. They are in the world 'directly', not by inhering in matter or qualifying an object. It might perhaps be a (philosophical) commonsense expectation that Anaxagoras would think of the Opposites as qualifying matter; but I submit that this is not the case. There are numerous reasons that make it plausible to hold that Anaxagoras's ontology does not include matter, as a substratum underlying the properties. First, an argument *ex silentio*: matter is never mentioned in the extant fragments.[14] Second, in a world where stuffs are metaphysically

---

[13] In the inventory of what there is in Anaxagoras's world there are seeds too, as we saw in B4b. What are they? The answer is not uncontroversial among scholars; but it does not bear significantly on the question of what metaphysics of properties Anaxagoras holds. For present purposes, we can take the example provided in B10, animal seed, as an instance of what Anaxagoras means when talking of seeds in general; from B10 we learn that the seeds are made out of stuffs, such as nail, hair, bone and so on. But stuffs are made out of Opposites. Thus, neither stuffs nor seeds are fundamental, for they are composed from Opposites and thus derivatives from them. Why does Anaxagoras include seeds in his ontology and for what purpose? Again, scholars disagree, but the question does not affect how we understand his metaphysics of properties. I contend that seeds are for Anaxagoras physical structures, around which the Opposites can cluster according to certain asymmetric patterns that explain the asymmetry of certain entities derivative from the Opposites (e.g. an organism, in contrast to a lump of earth).

[14] This cannot of course be a decisive argument by itself, for Anaxagoras's work has not been preserved in its entirety.

reducible to compresent properties (as we saw with the example of earth, in B15), Anaxagoras would have no motivation to hold that Opposites qualify some sort of material substratum that underlies them as their bearer. Third, *if* Anaxagoras thought that the Opposites were en-mattered in a sort of substratum, it would be historically odd that Plato or Aristotle do not engage at all with Anaxagoras's view of matter, in the *Timaeus* or the *Physics*, respectively. It was not until his later work that Plato introduced the notion of a 'Receptacle' of properties (which serves to locate copies of the Forms, as I will argue – but not the Forms themselves, which are unique in their own ontological domain); and subsequently Aristotle developed his theory of matter (more on these issues in Section 4). In conclusion, Anaxagoras has no reason to posit any type of entity like matter as underlying the Opposites.[15] Rather, the Opposites are particular properties in space and time, which do not qualify underlying characterless substrata of any kind, but which are primitively and eternally present in the world. *Properties first*, in Anaxagoras's ontology.

2.2 Parts of Properties/Parts of Objects

The Opposites are irreducible and thus fundamental entities in Anaxagoras's system, while material objects are derivative. Objects derive from concentrations of the Opposites in certain regions of space. In this sense, Anaxagoras holds an *ante litteram* Bundle Theory of things. Different theories of properties make for different versions of the Bundle Theory in modern philosophy. Modern bundle theorists, for the most part, endorse the view that properties exist as 'tropes', namely as particulars. On the trope version of the Bundle Theory, objects are bundles of tropes. As we saw, Anaxagoras's position aligns, broadly speaking, with this version of the theory, but with two very significant differences from the modern version. From the fact that the Opposites (their parts) can change spatial location, it follows that they are not individuated by the objects they qualify; they are 'transferable' from one object to another.[16] In this respect, Anaxagoras's conception of the Opposites differs from the mainstream way of individuating tropes in modern philosophy by the particular object they are properties of (e.g. Socrates's heat); such tropes are non-transferable properties.[17]

---

[15] For a discussion of alternative interpretations and a fuller discussion of mine, see Marmodoro 2017, section 1.2.

[16] Strictly speaking, it is not the Opposites that move anywhwere; it is rather their parts that move, come together and separate. Each Opposite is omnipresent in the cosmos, but its parts are preponderant in some locations. See the immediately following discussion.

[17] See for example Maurin (2022: 49) for more on tropes as conceived in modern metaphysics. No full account of what makes possible for Opposites to be moved spatially has survived, if Anaxagoras gave one. We take it at face value that the cosmic vortex can move Opposites in space.

Furthermore, a key presupposition of Anaxagoras is that the Opposites have parts. We are familiar with the idea that material objects have parts, but not with the idea that properties have parts, which are individuated independently of the objects which they constitute. Yet, recall that we have assumed that Anaxagoras's Opposites are physical entities, in the sense in which, for example, a magnetic field is physical, but not material. A magnetic field has parts: its sub-fields. This example can guide us in thinking about the parts of Anaxagoras's Opposites. We will return to the parts–whole relation within an Opposite later in this section (and also in relation to Plato's Forms, in Section 3). For now, I want to underscore the significance of what we have learned so far about Anaxagoras's metaphysics of properties. In his system, parts of Opposites are parts of objects, in the sense of constituting them. Thus (Opposite) properties and objects *overlap constitutionally*; for example the Opposite Hot and this hot pot share parts of the Hot between them, in the way that my glass of San Pellegrino water overlaps with the underground reservoir of San Pellegrino Terme. (This stance, as I will argue in Section 3, will be deeply influential on Plato's thought, and is key to understanding Plato's theory of participation in Forms.) We will see in what follows that for the Opposites to play the metaphysical role he gives them, Anaxagoras must be positing the following parts–whole relations: (i) the Opposites are unlimitedly divided into parts; and (ii) their parts are of the same kind as the whole of which they are parts; namely the Opposites are *homoeomers* (to use a term coined by Aristotle).

i. The Opposites exist as unlimitedly divided into parts

Abiding by a fundamental Parmenidean principle, namely that there is no passage from being to non-being and vice versa, Anaxagoras wants his system to allow that anything can 'come out' of anything, without creation *ex nihilo*, destruction of what there is, or qualitative change. To achieve this in his ontology, he posits that *everything is in everything* in nature (see B1, B6, B11, B12; see also Section 2.4): anything can 'come out' of anything, because it was already in it. In other words, change is nothing other than aggregation and separation of Opposites.[18]

What type of ontology could make it possible for everything to be in everything? Any ontology that posited indivisibles at the fundamental level of

---

[18] B17: 'The Greeks do not think correctly about coming-to-be and passing-away; for no thing comes to be or passes away, but is mixed together and dissociated from the things that are. And thus they would be correct to call coming-to-be being mixed together and passing-away being dissociated.'

kinds would thereby set a limit, below which it would not be the case that everything is in everything, and therefore, 'generation' and 'change' (as Anaxagoras conceives them) could not happen. This is something Anaxagoras does not want. For him, reality must be atom-less, with no indivisibles. Thus, the Opposites must be such as to be unlimitedly *divided* into parts, smaller and smaller ones, as per what I call Anaxagoras's *No Least Principle*, which I state thus:

No Least-P: There is no lowest limit to the magnitude of parts of Opposites.

Textual evidence to the effect that Anaxagoras endorses this principle can be found for instance in B1 and B3. In B3, Anaxagoras offers the example of the Opposite Small, as a kind that exists divided in unlimitedly small parts: 'Nor of the small is there a smallest, but always a smaller.' He also gives a justification for why the unlimited division of something into smaller and smaller parts does not lead to its elimination, that is to non-being: 'for what-is cannot not be', in line with the Parmenidean stance of no destruction *ad nihilum*, which Anaxagoras endorses. Therefore, from the *No Least-P* follows that every part of an Opposite divides into unlimitedly many parts.[19] The Opposites are not potentially divisible into parts that have parts and so on *ad infinitum*; rather, they are actually divided into parts that have parts and so on *ad infinitum*. We can infer this from B1, where Anaxagoras writes that 'All things were together, unlimited both in multitude and in smallness.' The fact that Opposites are actually divided facilitates their extreme mixture with one another, and therefore their distribution everywhere in the cosmos (discussed in Section 2.4).[20]

ii. The Opposites are homoeomers

Furthermore, Anaxagoras's Opposites are *homoeomers*, as Aristotle puts it in his *Physics* (203a19), coining a technical term specifically to refer to Anaxagoras's position; a *homoeomer* is such that its parts are all of the same kind as the whole of which they are parts is. Elsewhere, in the *De Generatione et Corruptione*, Aristotle gives as examples of *homoeomers* certain types of mixtures, and stuff like water: '. . . any part of such a compound is the same as the whole, just as any

---

[19] For Anaxagoras, each Opposite, for example the Hot, is the open set that includes all the parts of the Opposite in cosmos. The set is open because of Anaxagoras's *No Largest Principle*, expressed in B3 with *No Largest-P*: There is no upper limit to the magnitude of the opposites. (I formulate the principle thus in Marmodoro 2017, section 2.3 of chapter 2.) From this principle, it follows that any set corresponding to an extentional definition of an Opposite is open.

[20] On the location, omnipresence and preponderance of the Opposites in the cosmos, see Marmodoro (2015, and 2017, chapter 4), where I also present my account of Anaxagoras's *qualitative gunk*.

part of water is water' (328a10-12).[21] Although the examples given by Aristotle
are of material entities, the concept applies to non-material physical entities too,
like the Opposites, for example any part of the Hot is hot, as the Hot is, and so
forth. This feature of the Opposites facilitates their role of qualifying an object
as *f* by the presence of parts of F in them, all of which parts, at any level of
division, are of the same kind as F. More on this to follow.

2.3 The *Contagion Principle*

Anaxagoras's conception of how the Opposites 'make' something be qualified in
certain ways reveals to us a more general idea that was widespread in antiquity.
I call it the *Contagion Principle* of causation.[22] This principle is underpinned by
the thought that 'like causes like': *x* causes *y* to be like *x* itself (with respect
to *f-ness*). All that the *Contagion Principle* requires, in its most general formula-
tion, is the existence of a source (*x*) which itself possesses a certain condition
(*f-ness*), from which other things (e.g. *y*) somehow 'contract' it: *x*, which is itself *f*,
is the source of *y*'s *f-ness*. On the *Contagion Principle* the *f-ness* of an object is
traced back to a source of *f-ness* (hence, more broadly, to a 'sufficient reason' for
the object's *f-ness*).

The *Contagion Principle* can be thought of as a 'mechanism' for the *One over
Many Principle*, if it is assumed that the ultimate source of *f-ness* is unique (where
f-ness is a type of property). Such a mechanism explains how an ultimate source
of *f-ness* can make things be *f-similar* to each other: each thing acquires the
condition of being *f* from the source; and all things have the same condition of *f-ness*, because they acquire it from the same single source.

However, how the transmission of *f-ness* happens from the source to a thing
may be conceived of in different ways.[23] On Anaxagoras's account, *f-ness* is
transmitted from the source to other things by literal spatial transmission of parts
of the source – parts of Opposite F – to other things. The idea of spatial
transmission is intuitive in Anaxagoras's case, because the Opposites are physical
entities in the world.[24] Thus, Anaxagoras has an explanation to offer for how

---

[21] All translations of Aristotle's works (unless otherwise specified) are from Barnes (1984).

[22] Many in the history of philosophy have discussed this principle, each formulating it in their own
way; and many scholars of ancient philosophy also have interpreted it in different ways in
relation to how the ancients formulated it.

[23] More generally, the *Contagion Principle* entails that the condition contracted from the source,
f-ness, makes a difference to the constitution of the object contracting it, so that contagion is not
merely an external relation to the contracting object.

[24] The *Contagion Principle* does not presuppose the (Aristotelian) interactive process of efficient
causation; thus metaphysical systems like that of Anaxagoras devoid of (Aristotelian) causal
interaction can abide by the principle with no incoherence. To illustrate, hot coal may be
trasferred to a stove, thus making it hot by the presence of something hot *in* that stove, not by
heating the stove, which would be Aristotelian causal interaction.

f-ness is transmitted from the source; and its explanation has appeal within a system like his, where the Opposites are physical, have physical parts and may be spatially moved. The *Contagion Principle* is foundational for Plato's metaphysics too, as we will see in Section 3. However, there are important differences in their respective understanding of the principle: while Anaxagoras's Opposites are physical entities in the cosmos, Plato's Forms are transcendent entities; accordingly, the relation between a property and the thing it qualifies in the cosmos, respectively, is importantly different.

Before concluding this section, I would like to comment on how the *Contagion Principle* explains similarilty. We saw earlier in this section that the key concept is the oneness of the source of *f-ness*, which entails the sameness of the 'contracted' qualitative state. So, x and y are similar if they both acquire their qualitative state from the same source. This principle is firmly at the core of the ancients' thinking about similarity. However, it is also intuitive to think that x and y are similar if their qualitative state is the same, for example they are both red. This is a different and in a sense competing principle in relation to the *Contagion Principle* and it is also present in the ancient accounts of similarity, emerging clearly for example in Plato's work. In consequence, there are two distinct routes for accounting for similarity available to the ancients: either by claiming that x and y obtain their qualitative condition from the same source, or that their condition is the same. I anticipate here that these different and arguably equally intuitive explanations of similarity, both implementing the *One over Many Principle*, will generate problems for Plato, for example in the *Third Man Argument* (as we will see in Section 3.4).

2.4 Property Qualification

We saw that Anaxagoras assumes that physical properties such as the Hot, the Dry, the Cold and so on are literal constituents of things in the world: the parts of the Opposites make up things; in this sense, Opposites and things overlap constitutionally. Two assumptions underpin Anaxagoras's account: all Opposites are *homoeomers* and are divided 'all the way down' into unlimitedly many parts; *qua homoeomers*, the parts are of the same kind as the whole of which they are parts.[25] Next, we want to examine a further aspect of Anaxagoras's ontology, namely how objects are qualified by properties. One of his key principles, the so-called *Everything in Everything Principle*, claims that

---

[25] One may question whether Anaxagoras thought that such Opposites as the Large and the Small are properties, alongside the Wet and the Hot. The evidence from Anaxagoras's texts is not sufficient to decide, but my reasons for counting them as properties is that for Plato, who, I have argued in Marmodoro (2021), followed Anaxagoras in many respects in his ontology, the Large and the Small are Forms, alongside such Forms as the Hot.

EE-P: There is a part of everything in everything.[26]

This principle is explicitly stated and repeatedly mentioned in the extant texts of Anaxagoras, with different formulations (for instance in B1, B4b, B6, B12 and B12). I take the view (by no means shared by all interpreters) that the two occurrences of 'everything' in Anaxagoras's statement of *EE-P* are co-referring, and have the Opposites as their referents.[27] The Opposites exist only mixed with each other, and inseparable one from the other (for their inseparability, see for example B8).

However, how are things qualitatively differentiated in a world where everything is a mixture of everything? Anaxagoras's answer is that, in some things, there is 'more' of some Opposite(s) than there is of other Opposites. So, things are qualitatively different on account of which Opposites are preponderant in each thing. This is known in the literature as Anaxagoras's *Preponderance Principle*, which I state thus:

P-P: A thing is *f* if and only if the Opposite F is preponderant in that thing's constitution (in relation to other Opposites also present in the thing).

P-P explains why things are qualified by certain Opposites (e.g. as being hot) and are of a certain kind (e.g. silver or earth), even if all things contain all the Opposites. As we saw in Section 2.2, the Opposites are literally everywhere in the cosmos, and have unlimitedly many parts, which are all of the same kind as the Opposite of which they are parts. Yet, there is more of them[28] in certain regions of the cosmos, qualifiying objects in a certain way. In Anaxagoras's own

[26] Interpreters have been traditionally divided on whether the Opposites are present in the extreme mixture of everything in everything as very small *particles*, or as very small *proportions* of each type of thing. These are respectively labelled in the literature, the *particulate* and the *proportionate* interpretations. According the first of the two, Anaxagoras is thinking of juxtaposed particles of stuff; according to the other, he is thinking of proportions of stuff in a mixture. On the particulate interpretation, the material elements of Anaxagoras's ontology are present as such in the mixture, as material particles of finite size that are too small to be perceptually discerned; so they appear mixed throughout. On the proportionate interpretation on the other hand, the total quantity of each type of material element is mixed together with the total quantities of the rest of the elements, so that the totality is a uniform mixture through and through. I argued elsewhere that both lines of interpretation (as well as the third alternative put forward by Curd as the so-called *liquids model*) are prey to serious difficulties, philosophical and/or textual ones. My thesis is that the Opposites are not containing each other; rather, they are *compresent* with each other. For Anaxagoras there is a part of everything *with* everything, rather than a part of everything contained *in* everything. See Marmodoro (2017) chapters 3 and 4.
[27] Some interpretaters hold that 'everything' has the same referent in both occurrences (see for instance Guthrie (1969: 284–5); others, notably Sedley, argue that the referent is not and cannot be the same (2007: 29–30). I have given arguments for my view in Marmodoro (2017, section 2.2 of chapter 2).
[28] I addressed the issue of how there can be more parts somewhere of something that has unlimitedly many parts everywhere in Marmodoro (2017), section 3.6 of chapter 3.

words, in B1: 'all things being in everything, but each being characterized by what predominates'. In B12 also:

> Nothing else is like anything else, but each one is and was most manifestly those things of which there are the most in it.

So if an Opposite is preponderant in relation to the other Opposites in a location, it is most manifest there, that is it is perceptually evident; and the location wherein it is appears to be of that kind to us, for example hot, dry, bright. I call this Anaxagoras's *Distributive Model* of qualification, whereby an Opposite can qualify many objects in the world by being distributed to them through its parts, if its parts are preponderant in relation to other Opposites in these objects.

What is Anaxagoras's metaphysical mechanism for preponderance? Also, is he thinking of preponderance in quantity or in intensity of the parts of an Opposite? For instance, is a fire hot because there are more parts of the Hot in it, or because the parts of Hot in it are very hot? Both interpretations of *P-P*, in terms of quantitative preponderance or of higher intensity, are consistent with the other metaphysical commitments of Anaxagoras, and either way, the mechanism that produces preponderance is by accumulation and dispersal of the parts of the Opposites.[29]

To take stock: for Anaxagoras, properties – the Opposites – are 'directly' in the world. Objects are in the world on account of the properties/Opposites that make them up, overlapping constitutionally with them. Properties are fundamental, objects derivative. It is important to highlight that while an object is constituted of all the Opposites, it is qualified only by the Opposites whose parts are preponderant within its constitution. I contend that Anaxagoras pioneers a distinction that will be very influential on how his successors, Plato and Aristotle, developed their metaphysics of properties: the distinction between *being part of* an object and *qualifying* the object. However, this distinction for Anaxagoras is merely quantitative. The qualification of an object by an Opposite is due to its having within its constitution 'more presence' or preponderance of that Opposite in relation to other Opposites. Anaxagoras has nothing further to offer, in the extant fragments at least, to differentiate metaphysically being a part from being a qualification of an object. As we will see in Section 4, this distinction is of fundamental metaphysical importance to Aristotle; Plato before him is already philosophically troubled by the concern that the mere presence of a property in an object is not apt to explain how the property qualifies the object. In the *Lysis*, Plato introduces what we would consider

---

[29] See Marmodoro (2017 section 2.5. of chapter 2).

a thought experiment that teases apart presence of a property from property qualification, thus:

> 'Look at it this way' I said 'If someone smeared your blond hair with white lead, would your hair then *be* white or *appear* white?' 'Appear white', he said. 'And yet whiteness would surely be *present* with it.' 'Yes.' 'But all the same your hair would not yet be white. Though whiteness would be *present*, your hair *would not be* white any more than it is black.' 'True.' (217d1-6; emphasis in the original translation)

Plato's explicit stance here appears to be a direct rejection of Anaxagoras's stance that objects are qualified by what is merely present in them. Plato even builds his example so as to secure that the white colour would be preponderant in the hair – which satisfies Anaxagoras's *P-P*. Plato concludes:

> 'But when, my friend, old age introduces this same color [white] to your hair, then it will *become* of the same sort as what is *present*, white by the presence of white.' 'Naturally.' 'Here at last is my question, then. When a thing has something *present* with it, will it be of the *same sort* [white] as what is present? Or only when that thing is *present in a certain way* [by *belonging as a property* to the subject]?' 'Only then', he said. (217d6-e4; my emphasis)

Does Plato offer an argument, here, against the thought that the mere presence of properties in objects qualifies the objects with those properties? He does not; but he makes an observation of great significance for the history of philosophy, taking forward Anaxagoras's original intuition that *being part of* an object is different from *qualifying* an object. For Anaxagoras, the difference was that preponderance was required for qualification. Plato here says that *belonging as a property* to an object is different from merely *being present in* that object. For Plato, this is a more challenging philosophical position, because for at least part of his career, as we will see in Section 3, he holds that a property qualifies an object by being merely present in the object (through a part of the property in the object's constitution). We will see in Section 4 how Aristotle takes Plato's thinking forward.

2.5 Qualitative Similarity

Are the parts of Anaxagoras's Opposite Hot hot? Aristotle thought so; he called Anaxagoras's Opposites *homoeomers*, as we saw in Section 2.2. Anaxagoras did provide a general metaphysical explanation of property qualification, which applies also to parts of the Opposites. For him, asking whether the parts of the Hot are hot is asking whether the parts of the Hot have in them a preponderance of parts of the Hot (which is also what makes the Hot hot). 'Being hot' is not a qualitative state in Anaxagoras's metaphysics, as it is in Aristotle's, but a quantitative state. So, the question arises: in virtue of what are the parts of the Hot similar between them, for Anaxagoras? As just stated, they are not similar in virtue of a qualitative state of being hot, but rather in virtue of their quantitative state: not by suchness, but by preponderance. The same answer applies to all the Opposites, because the parts of each Opposite are similar to that Opposite, respectively, by having a preponderance of parts of that Opposite within them; so the parts of the Opposite Hot are similar to the Hot because they each have a preponderance of parts of the Hot in them, and so forth *ad infinitum*. This is what it is for the parts of an Opposite to be similar betwen them, and to the Opposite; this is what it is for them to be *homoeomers*. It follows that Anaxagoras's Opposites must be *primitively* different from each other; that is, their difference cannot be explained in his metaphysics, because his system does not reify the qualitative aspects of each of the different Opposites.

2.6 Conclusion

Anaxagoras made a number of very significant contributions to metaphysics. Here I want to highlight possibly the most influential: he explained the being of stuffs and objects in nature in terms of properties. (Recall for example B15 about the constitution of earth.) Before him, the ontology of things in nature had been explained in terms of material stuff, such as water or air. Even though Anaxagoras's properties, his Opposites, are physical, located in nature, and *homoeomeric* like stuffs (e.g. water or air), nevertheless his stance that things are constituted of properties must have been a highly counterintuitive position at his time (possibly comparable in our times to the discovery that solid objects are mostly empty 'inside'?). Furthermore, Anaxagoras introduced a *Distributive Model* to explain qualification and similarity in terms of the parts of Opposite properties, which, as we will see, will be adopted by Plato in his theory of Forms and participation. Anaxagoras was the first philosopher to distinguish between an object's *having a part of* an Opposite property, and the object *being qualified by* the Opposite. We will see that both Plato and Aristotle will develop theories that take this distinction forward into much more sophisticated metaphysical accounts than what we find in Anaxagoras, whose model was merely quantitative; nevertheless, his original insight was a paradigm shift in metaphysics.

3 Plato's Forms

While the mutual philosophical influence between Plato and Aristotle has been the object of much investigation ever since their immediate successors, with Aristotle himself punctuating his metaphysical works with references to Plato (and their disagreements), much less investigated and understood, I contend, is the extent to which Plato was deeply influenced by Anaxagoras. There are ancient testimonies, textual evidence and philosophical reasons that all point in this direction. The case has been argued by, for example, Brentingler (1972), Denyer (1983), Mann (2000), Forciganò (2019) and Marmodoro (2021), among others. Numerous considerations support this interpretation of Plato's theory of Forms and of participation as influenced by Anaxagoras. To start with, there are references in ancient sources that point to a derivative connection between Plato's and Anaxagoras's metaphysics of participation of objects in properties. We know from Aristotle (*Met.* 991a14-19) and Alexander of Aphrodisias (*In Met.* 97, 27-98, 24) that Eudoxos in particular offered an interpretation of Plato's theory in Anaxagorean terms. Furthermore, Plato's language in speaking of participation as μετέχειν is clearly of Anaxagorean origin. However, the decisive reasons for interpreting Plato's theory of participation (at least before what I consider his fresh start in the *Timaeus*)[30] as Anaxagorean are philosophical, rather than historical, testimonial or linguistic; we will discuss them in this section.

Both Anaxagoras and Plato (albeit with significant differences, as we will see) conceive of things in the world as partaking of properties according to the *Distributive Model*, in the sense of literally having parts of the properties within their constitution, and thus *overlapping constitutionally* with them. I will show that Plato sees the explanatory value of Anaxagoras's stance that properties are parts/constituents of things. Plato however aims to combine his own theory of properties, which differs significantly from Anaxagoras's, with Anaxagoras's account of participation. Plato finds much to be gained, philosophically, from this approach; but, as we will see, he also reaches the limit of the explanatory power of Anaxagoras's metaphysics when extending it further than Anaxagoras did.

Ultimately, Plato abandons his Anaxagorean account of participation and turns to a different one, motivated by the difficulties he discovers in trying to combine his theory of Forms with Anaxagoras's theory of participation by distribution of parts. On Plato's alternative account, which I call the *Mimetic Model*, Forms are 'imitated' by the sensible particulars, which become imperfect copies of the Forms that qualify them. While Plato had the *Mimetic Model* under consideration throughout his dialogues, as we know for example from the *Parmenides*[31] and the *Republic* (e.g. in what I call the *Third Bed Argument*

---

[30] I offer arguments for why I consider the *Timaeus* a fresh start in Plato's thought in Marmodoro (2021), chapter 7 in particular.

[31] See for example the *Parmenides*: '[...] what appears most likely to me is this: these forms are like patterns set in nature, and other things resemble them and are likenesses of them; and this partaking of the forms is, for the other things, simply being modeled on them' (132d1-4).

(TBA); see Section 3.3), it will not be until the *Timaeus* that he will make it his preferred model, having found insurmountable difficulties with the *Distributive Model*. In the *Timaeus*, Plato also enriches the *Mimetic Model* by introducing the operation of a divine agent, the *Demiurge*, as an efficient cause, to implement imitation. The *Demiurge* (and other semi-gods) copy the Forms, which are embodied in the so-called *paradeigma* – an *über* Form that comprises all the Forms. When the Demiurge fashions the individual objects in nature by selecting and copying the relevant Forms (now conceived as aspects of the *paradeigma*), such objects become qualified with the corresponding properties. Imitation is a metaphorical (and metaphysically opaque) way of accounting for participation in a property; metaphysically speaking, neither imitation nor the *Demiurge*'s intermediation are philosophical improvements on the original Anaxagorean *Distributive Model*, towards accounting for property possession. Since the *Mimetic Model* will not be influential in the history of philosophy, we will not discuss it in detail here. In between the *Distributive* and the *Mimetic Model*, Plato interestingly is the first to conceive and explore what will become Aristotle's *forte*: the *Recurrence Model* – to this we will give careful consideration in this section.

3.1 Plato's Forms vis-à-vis Anaxagoras's Opposites

There are two fundamental tenets of Anaxagoras that Plato agrees with: the primacy of properties in the ontology, and the *Contagion Principle* of explanation. Plato's Forms, like Anaxagoras's Opposites, are sources from which *f-ness* is transmitted to things in such a way that *f-ness* becomes part of their constitution. In general, the *Contagion Principle* assumes that sameness derives from oneness; so, being in the same *f*-condition presupposes having derived *f-ness* from the same one source. In Plato's system, and in full accordance with the *Contagion Principle*, a thing is *f* if it 'contracts' the *f*-condition that Form F stands for, by partaking in the Form F (the source); and two things are *f*-similar if they 'contract' their *f*-condition from the same source, by partaking of one and the same Form F.

There are however significant divergences between Plato's and Anaxagoras's theories of properties. We saw in Section 1 that Anaxagoras posits physical Opposites as the building blocks of his system – opposite natural properties (such as the Cold and the Wet). Plato has a more 'expansive' approach; he includes in his ontology of properties physical opposites, but also further types of opposites, such as moral and aesthetic values (e.g. justice, beauty), and even kinds (being a human being, being a bed, etc.), which are not opposites. In some contexts, Plato's criterion for positing Forms appears liberal to the point of

encompassing the referents of all predicates in language, if we take at face value
what he writes in the *Republic*:

> As you know, we customarily hypothesize a single form in connection with
> each of the many things to which we apply the same name. (596a)

On this criterion, a single Form is posited for each group of entities we classify
together in the world of our experience, the 'many', to which we apply the same
name (i.e. predicate, for example being hot).

In addition to expanding the range of types of properties admitted into the
ontology, Plato makes another, much more significant departure from
Anaxagoras. Plato conceives of the Forms as transcendent entities, existing in
'a place beyond the heaven' (see for example *Phaedrus* 247 c, *Republic* 517b-c).
Plato 'elevates' the status of Anaxagoras's physical Opposites to that of
non-physical and intelligible entities, whose presence in material objects, nevertheless, qualifies the objects as f (as being thus-and-so, for example hot). This
choice does not sit well with the Anaxagorean *Distributive Model*; the outcome of
combining that model with Plato's ontology of properties is a surprising one:
material objects are, for example, hot, by having within their constitution a part of
the Form of Heat, which is a transcendent property! This raises the problem of
how transcendent properties can constitute material objects. Eventually, Plato will
choose a different model of participation, the *Mimetic Model*, which avoids the
problem of material objects being constituted of (parts of) transcendent properties, even if it raises the problem of how material objects can resemble (by
imitation) transcendent entities.

Furthermore, we saw that Anaxagoras's Opposites are particular;
a commonplace among scholars and contemporary philosophers alike is that
Plato's Forms are universals, as mentioned in Section 1.5; if so, this would be
a further and very significant difference between Anaxagoras and Plato.
Interpreters however are not unanimous: some have argued that the Forms are
universals (see for example G. Fine 1993 and Harte 2008, among many others),
and some that they are particular (I have, in Marmodoro 2021). Certainly, each
Form qualifies multiple individuals that partake of it (hence it is universal in this
specific sense); but it can do so while being a particular, as Anaxagoras's
Opposites do, by distribution of parts. It is my contention that Plato (at least
before the *Timaeus*) endorses Anaxagoras's model of the universalisation of
a property by distribution of its parts (rather than by the recurrence of the
property, which is Aristotle's model). I will show that Plato argues explicitly
against the recurrence of Forms, in what I call the *Partaking Dilemma* (examined here in Section 3.2). However, Plato also finds difficulties in the idea that
parts of the Forms can serve metaphysically as 'proxies' of the Forms that

qualify objects and ground their similarities. He examines these difficulties on different occasions in his work, namely in the *Partaking Dilemma* (here in Section 3.2), and in the *Third Man Argument* (TMA) (here in Section 3.4). The difficulties arise from the tension between a Form being unique, but also being many, because functionally equivalent to its many parts (with respect to the metaphysical work it does).

In what I call TBA (here in Section 3.3), Plato hypothesises the possibility that properties recur (in Aristotelian sense) in his system – although he does not ultimately pursue the idea further. Such recurrence does not multiply the recurring entity, which is uniquely one, but only its occurrence. Importantly, as we will see, in Plato's thought experiment it is the 'forms of Forms', as he puts it (the *essences* of Forms, in Aristotelian terminology) that recur, not the Forms themselves. Plato however shows philosophical awareness that, if there were essences of Forms in his system, that is, if a Form were what it is on account of something else, that is, its essence, very significant difficulties would arise, which he develops in the TMA.[32]

3.2 The *Partaking Dilemma*

Numerous considerations, as we saw, support the interpretation of Plato's theory of Forms and participation as influenced by Anaxagoras. One of these considerations is that Plato discusses often and in depth in his dialogues the position that properties qualify objects by having their parts distributed to the partaking objects, along the lines of Anaxagoras's *Distributive Model*. (Anaxagoras is hardly ever mentioned by name by Plato in such contexts, but this is in line with how the ancients often discussed each other's views.) Plato scrutinises the position and, as we will see below, engages with the difficulties arising for his theory of Forms.

An important context where Plato examines Anaxagoras's *Distributive Model* as problematic is the *Parmenides*, by means of what I call the *Partaking Dilemma*. The *Dilemma* is relevant both to the question of whether Forms are universal or particular, and to the question of how Forms are 'in' objects. In the *Dilemma*, Plato considers two ways in which a Form can be present in an object: by the object having the whole of a Form in it, or by the object having a part of a Form in it. We read:

> 'So does each thing that gets a share get as its share the Form as a whole, or a part of it? Or could there be some other means of getting a share apart from these two?' 'How could there be?' he said. (131a)

---

[32] Which Aristotle blocks in *Metaphysics* Z.6, to avoid an *Essence Regress* from developing, as we will see in Section 4.5.

The argument allows for only two ways of participating in a Form: either the whole Form occurs in the partaking things, or parts of the Form are distributed to partaking things. Both ways will turn out to be metaphysically problematic for Plato. If the Form F is present as a whole in every *f*-thing, then it follows that the Form F is different from itself, in its various simultaneous occurences in the *f*-objects. If, on the other hand, it is only a part of the Form F that is present in every *f*-thing (by distribution of the parts of the Form), the problem is that the parts of a Form would serve as metaphysical 'proxies' of the Form, thereby multiplying the Form, which is *One over Many*.

Let us consider in more detail the latter horn of the *Dilemma*, which investigates the hypothesis that Forms are distributed in parts. Plato writes:

> 'For suppose you are going to divide largeness itself. If each of the many large things is to be large by a part of largeness smaller than largeness itself, won't that appear unreasonable?' 'It certainly will', he replied. 'What about this? Will each thing that has received a small part of the equal have something by which to be equal to anything, when its portion is less than the equal itself?' 'That's impossible.' (131c-d)

The question Plato is raising is this: can the parts of a Form do the metaphysical work that the Form as a whole would do, namely qualifying objects with the property the Form stands for? If they could, the result would be that a From is not unique, *contra* the TBA's conclusion, but is as many as its parts. Plato finds it 'unreasonable' that the parts could do the metaphysical work that the Form does, as we see in the text quoted above. The absurdity is illustrated with the example of a part of Largeness, which is *small* (smaller than Largeness itself), and yet, *per hypothesis*, would qualify the object it is in as *large* (thus violating the principle that 'like causes like', introduced here in Section 2.3). I take the *Partaking Dilemma* to apply to the way an object participates in any Form. So we need to understand the metaphysical problem in its generality. Why can a large object not be large by virtue of a part of the Form of Largeness, notwithstanding the fact that the part, *qua* part, is 'smaller than' the Form of Largeness as a whole? How are we to understand the key idea in this argument, that, for any Form F, the 'smallness' of a part of F in relation to the whole F renders problematic how a part of F qualifies an object as *f*?

Liddell and Scott distinguish three senses of σμικρός in their Greek-English Lexicon, the third of which is 'small in importance' or significance, which is cognate to being less impactful,[33] and thus less effective or less powerful. This meaning seems the relevant one here. I suggest that Plato's thought in the *Partaking Dilemma* is that a part of a Form cannot be functionally equivalent to the whole Form.

---

[33] Plato uses the term with this meaning for example in *Republic* 473b3-c1.

Why should parts be functionally inadequate for the metaphysical role that Plato hypothesises they can play, namely of distributing the property of the Form to the many, and qualifying them by being present in them? Plato does not explain the inadequacy of parts of Forms here, but he does state the *adequacy* of Forms for qualifying objects. In the first horn of the *Dilemma*, Plato assumes that an object *would be* qualified as *f* by having the whole of Form F in it; the problem Plato finds with this proposal is that Forms cannot be whole in many objects (and thus explain similarity). The reason is given in a brief but important exchange following the *Dilemma*:

> 'Do you think, then, that the Form as a whole – one thing – is in each of the many?'
> 'What's to prevent it being one, Parmenides?' said Socrates.
> 'So, being one and the same, it will be at the same time, as a whole, in things that are many and separate; and, thus it would be separate from itself.'
> (131a-b)

I reconstruct Plato's reasoning as follows. The Form F is what stands for the property of being *f*, whose presence in an object qualifies the object as *f*. Thus, if there are two hot things in the world, each of them must have the Form of Heat in them to be qualified as hot. But, *per hypothesis*, only the whole Form can qualify an object with the property of being hot. Furthermore, there is only one Form per type of property (which Plato shows in the TBA; here in Section 3.3). From the assumption that objects require the presence of the whole Form in order to be qualified as *f*, and that each Form is unique, absurdities follow, namely that a Form would become different from itself, as mentioned in the text quoted above. This is why Plato assumes, in the second horn of the *Dilemma*, that the parts of a Form, being 'smaller' than the Form itself, are functionally inadequate for qualifying objects with the property the Form stands for. For, if the parts were functionally adequate for qualifying the many objects they are in, they would each be functioning as the Form itself, multiplying the Form. Plato rejects this on the ground that a part of a whole cannot do the metaphysical job that the whole of a Form can perform.

We are now in the position to draw two important conclusions from the *Partaking Dilemma*: that Plato considers and rejects the option of a Form as a recurring universal that is wholly present in multiple objects at once (because he thinks that since there is only one Form per type of property, to recur, the Form would have to be different from itself).[34] Furthermore, Plato finds serious

---

[34] A conjecture: we will see that Plato says in his TBA that the essence of a Form (f_3) *recurs* in different individuals. I will ask why Plato does not develop this into a theory of recurrent Forms, and will give metaphysical reasons explaining why. Does the *Parmenides* show us an additional reason Plato had? Could it be that Plato did not want Forms to be recurrent, precisely because he thought they would multiply as described here, and so a Form would be many? I believe there is much more that needs to be said about the *recurrence* of Forms, about the *duplication* of Forms

difficulties with the (Anaxagorean) idea that an object is qualified by a Form by having a part (or more parts, according to Anaxagoras) of the Form within its constitution, because Plato thinks that a part of the Form cannot be functionally equivalent to the Form of which it is a part. But if not by partaking of a Form, and overlapping constitutionally with it by having a part of it, how else can an object come to be qualified by a Form? The question remains open for now.

A further question arises for us from the *Dilemma*: on the first horn's hypothesis, if a Form is present as a whole in objects and thus is separate from itself (by duplication), does the Form recur? I want to distinguish *recurrence* from *duplication* of Forms, which is an important metaphysical distinction that has not been exhaustively discussed in the literature. Plato concludes the first horn of the *Dilemma* by claiming that a Form cannot recur because otherwise *ipso facto* it would get duplicated. But this does not follow, because recurrence and duplication are metaphysically different phenomena.

I contend that when Plato says in the *Dilemma* that a Form cannot recur in different objects because it would become different from itself, he is confusing duplication with recurrence.[35] Plato has not produced an argument against the recurrence of universals here,[36] because the occurrence of a Form in many things would not require the duplication of the Form, but only its recurrence in space.

Independently of what Plato thought, my claim, to reiterate it, is that duplication is different from recurring. I will explain what I mean, here: duplication is straighforward, it is like cloning something. However, recurrence is more challenging to comprehend. Typically, when we talk of a recurring universal property we mean that the property occurs whole in different objects in the world. Whereas duplication repeats the presence of an entity as such, recurrence allots multiply the presence of the entity in a dimension that the entity itself is not in.[37] Generally, a universal is not in space, and when it recurs in space (in many objects), it is one and the same entity that is multiply qualified with spatial properties (locations). For example, an Aristotelian universal, e.g. the redness of a rose that is *abstracted* from every red rose (and thereby from any spatial qualification), recurs

---

and about *recurrence* at large before we fully understand the problem Plato is struggling with here. I come back to recurrence and duplication in this section.

[35] On the other hand, the clearest example of duplication of properties is found in Plato's TBA (Section 3.3), where the Form of Bed is duplicated into F_1 and F_2. Admitttedly, the Form is duplicated *per impossibile*, but nevertheless the TBA shows that Plato understands duplication (F_1 and F_2) and recurrence (of f_3) as different phenomena.

[36] A further interesting observation to make is that Plato's argument in the *Dilemma* against the duplication of a Form would apply only to the TBA where f_3 needs to be duplicated, to occcur in all of F_1, F_2 and F_3, because they are all Forms.

[37] The difference between recurrence and duplication is to be investigated further in general, and also specifically with respect to what Plato may contribute to our understanding of it with his examples of the day and the sail in the *Parmenides* (at 131).

in many red roses by being qualified spatially in various ways; but it is *not* duplicated and is *not* different from itself, for the spatial dimension is not involved in the individuation of the universal, but it makes possible its recurrence (more on this in Section 4).

3.3 The *Third Bed Argument*

Plato puts forward in *Republic* X a thought experiment, concerning whether each Form is unique; this is the TBA.[38] Can there be more than one numerically different Form for each kind (e.g. two Forms of Heat)? Speaking generally, on account of the *Contagion Principle*, Plato can straightaway claim that if there were two qualitatively identical entities, they would have their common qualitative condition from the same source, which means that in addition to the two entities, a third one would have to be posited as their common source. However, the main general point I want to extract from this argument is that, as we will see, Plato assumes that the common qualitative condition that two qualitatively identical entities (per hypothesis) share is wholly present in each of them; it recurs in them! Here I will discuss the significance of this argument for the recurrence of universals. Importantly, what Plato claims in the TBA is *not* that Forms are universals, recurring in objects, but rather, and surprisingly, that *the form of each Form* recurs in the entities that partake of the Form. The argument runs as follows:

> [I] f he [god] made only two [Forms of Bed, F_1 and F_2], then again one [Form of Bed, F_3] would come to light whose form [τὸ εἶδος, f_3] they in turn would both possess, and *that* [Form F_3] would be the one that is the being of a bed, and not the other two [F_1 and F_2]. (597c)[39]

In brief, the thrust of the argument, as Plato sees it, is that there is, and there can be (by the *Contagion Principle* or its derivative *One over Many Principle*), only one Form F, in virtue of which *f*-similar things are similar, *qua* likenesses of the Form. If there were two Forms standing for the same type of property, F_1 and F_2, they would be, *per hypothesis*, qualitatively identical to one another, but also numerically different from each other, since they would be two. But if F_1 and F_2 were qualitatively identical but numerically different, they would be similar, and so they would both be similar in virtue of a further Form F_3 – the source – wherefrom their respective qualitative conditions derive. The ultimate explanation is that qualitative sameness is accounted for by the oneness of the source (F_3) of that

---

[38] For a detailed analysis of the TBA and the relevant scholarly literature, see Marmodoro (2008, 2021 and 2022a).

[39] Here it will be helpful to have the key line in the original: εἰ δύο μόνας ποιήσειεν, πάλιν ἂν μία ἀναφανείη ἧς ἐκεῖναι ἂν αὖ ἀμφότεραι τὸ εἶδος ἔχοιεν, καὶ εἴη ἂν ὃ ἔστιν κλίνη ἐκείνη ἀλλ᾽ οὐχ αἱ δύο.

qualitative condition. We would expect therefore their similarity to be explained by each partaking of F_3 by possessing a part of F_3; but this is not the case in the TBA. Rather, their similarity is explained by each of the two similar entities *possessing the very same entity*, namely the *form* of F_3 – call it f_3. Plato is explicit about this in the text: 'again one [Form] would come to light *whose form* they in turn would both possess' (597c).[40]

So, Plato's argument continues, (the new Form) F_3 will in fact be *the* Form of *f-ness*, while the originally hypothesised two Forms of *f-ness*, F_1 and F_2, will only be similar to F_3, but numerically different from it (by the thought experiment's hypothesis). As such, F_1 and F_2 fail to be Forms F according to Plato ('that [F_3] would be the one which is what "bed" really is, and *not* the other two'). Thus, there can be only one Form F, uniquely, which can qualify other items as *f*; or else, I add, we would not be able to explain the similarity between F_1 and F_2. This is the conclusion Plato draws, confirming the *Contagion Principle* and the *One over Many Principle*. But what we learn from the TBA is of broader philosophical significance for the history of metaphysics of properties.

We saw that Form F_3 is the Form required to explain the similarity of the two original Forms, F_1 and F_2, and qualifies both of them as *f*. The next step is critical: if F_1, F_2 and F_3 are all *f* (namely Forms of Bed, in the example at hand), what is the source of their *f-ness*? In the TMA (as we will see in Section 3.4), the answer would be that there is a further Form, F_4, which makes all three of them *f* (by all three of them partaking in F_4), which, however, generates a regress of Forms. Here in the TBA Plato's answer is importantly different. F_1, F_2 and F_3 are all *f* without partaking of a further Form, F_4; rather, each of them is *f* by possessing form f_3 – no regress, because not only does f_3 make each of them *f* but also it makes all of them *f*-similar to each other without partaking of further Forms. That is to say, f_3 is sufficient for both qualification and similarity of all *f*-things, which is why a TMA regress does not arise here. This is the explanatory advantage of a recurrent universal. Had Plato developed a theory of recurring universals after the TBA, no TMA could have been formulated.

---

[40] Here it will be helpful to have the key words in the original: ἧς ἐκεῖναι ἂν αὖ ἀμφότεραι τὸ εἶδος ἔχοιεν.

The metaphysical difference between form f_3 and Form F_3 is neither self-evident nor explained in the TBA. I will resist conjecturing, but in my understanding this difference is the reason why I do not think that Plato's Forms are universals – only the form of a Form (e.g. f_3) is a recurring universal in F_1 and F_2; F_3 does not recur (recall the *Partaking Dilemma*). In a sense, the recurrence of f_3 is a new 'mechanism' for the distribution of F_3, instead of by F_3's division into parts and distribution of the parts, or worse, instead of separating F_3 from itself. In this sense, the TBA shows that there are two *Ones* over Many: the Form, and the form of the Form.

Something further happens in the TBA as well, of great metaphysical significance. Plato does not seem to see it, but Aristotle will respond to it in what I call the *Essence Regress* in *Metaphysics* Z.6 (which we will touch upon in Section 3.4, and discuss in Section 4.5). In the TBA, Plato postulates the 'division' of a Form into a *subject* and its *essence* (to use Aristotelian terminology) – into the Form and the form of a Form (in Plato's terminology). This division is relevant to several aspects of Plato's theory of Forms, for example to the Self-Predication of Forms, and to the TMA Regress; more generally, to whether a Form F is *made f* by a substance-making relation that makes it what it is; and even more generally, to the problem of the oneness of a substance (Plato's Forms included), which is undermined by the subject–essence division.

3.4 The *Third Man Argument*

Before analysing the TMA in detail, let us formulate the core problem which Plato is uncovering through this argument. We saw that both Anaxagoras and Plato follow, in general, the *Contagion Principle*, whereby a thing 'contracts' its condition of being *f* from a source of *f-ness*, for example the Opposite O, or the Form F. Anaxagoras does not raise the question of the *f-ness* of an Opposite, which is treated as a primitive in his system. However, this leaves something unexplained by the *Contagion Principle*: the *f-ness* of the source of *f-ness*, which remains outside the explanatory remit of the principle. Plato does not settle for this, and puts the *Contagion Principle* to a test, by 'questioning' the *f-ness* of the source. The TMA testifies to the impossibility of, on the one hand, remaining faithful to the principle of explanation embodied in the *Contagion Principle* (always referring to a source of *f-ness*), while on the other hand, *additionally* explaining the *f-ness* of the source as well. (Aristotle too, in his *Essence Regress* in *Metaphysics* Z.6 (as we will see here in Section 4.5) examines the question of whether the *f-ness* of the source of *f-ness* (i.e. the *f-ness* of the *essence* of *f-ness*) should be explained. He blocks the regress that would ensue if an explanation were to be sought, by *fiat*, treating the *f-ness* of the source of *f-ness* as primitive.)

Furthermore, the TMA reveals an additional problem with the *Contagion Principle*. If similarity between two *f*-similar entities is explained by the *Contagion Principle* as their having the same source of *f-ness*, then the similarity between these *f*-things and their source of *f-ness* would require a further (common) source of *f-ness* to explain it (by the *Contagion Principle*), and so on *ad infinitum*. This last thought points to a contradiction between the conditions of *qualification* and of *similarity*, to which we will come below as the 'heart' of the TMA problems, and which is the ultimate and unavoidable (structural) problem undermining the *Contagion Principle* of explanation. I will show that after gaining understanding of how the *Contagion Principle* impacts on his theory of Forms in the TMA, Plato will reformulate the theory of Forms in the *Timaeus*, introducing primitive conditions, precisely to avoid the difficulties the *Contagion Principle* generates, and to block the TMA Regress. (I will claim that Plato's answer to the TMA in the *Timaeus* is the same as Aristotle's will be in his *Essence Regress*, as we will see: the *f-ness* of Form F is primitive.)

We saw in Section 2.3 that the *Contagion Principle* explains the cause of the qualitative state of an object by tracing it back to a source with that condition and from which the object acquired the condition. Turning to Plato's *Parmenides*, we find that

> there are certain forms from which these other things, by getting a share of
> them, derive their names – as, for instance, they come to be like by getting
> a share of likeness, large by getting a share of largeness, and just and beautiful
> by getting a share of justice and beauty. (130e-131a)

So there are *f*-things in the world (e.g. beautiful things, large things, things that are alike); they become *f* by partaking of Form F, which is what it is to be *f* (e.g. partaking of the Form of Beauty). Plato further states the *One over Many Principle* (with the example of Largeness):

> 'I suppose you think each form is one on the following ground: whenever
> some number of things seem to you to be large, perhaps there seems to be
> some one character, the same as you look at them all, and from that you
> conclude that the large is one.'
>   'That is true', he [Socrates] said. (132a)

So, for all *f*-things in the world, there is one Form F, which is the type *f-ness* and which is unique. However, since that Form F, which is the source of *f-ness* that 'spreads' its qualitative condition to *f*-things, is also *f*, given the *f*-things and Form F, all of which are *f*, by the same *One over Many Principle*, 'there seems to be some one character, the same as you look at them all', which Plato recognises:

> 'What about the large itself and the other large things? If you look at them all
> in the same way with the mind's eye, again, won't some one thing appear
> large, by which all these appear large?' 'It seems so.' (132a)

Nothing that Plato has said so far suggests that there is more than one Form of Largeness. We need additionally to assume that there are no universals to explain the similarity Plato describes (*à la* TBA). It is only in the following well-known conclusion of the TMA that Plato commits himself to needing an additional Form F to explain the *f*-similarity of a Form-F-and-all-other-*f*-things, which then generates the regress:

> So another form of largeness will make its appearance, which has appeared alongside largeness itself and the things that partake of it, and in turn another over all these, by which all of them will be large. Each of your forms will no longer be one, but unlimited in multitude. (132a-b, translation slightly modified)

I want to emphasise that only this last quotation shows which model of participation in Forms Plato is discussing here, which until this point in the argument was left open. We now learn that he is presupposing the *Distributive Model* rather than the *Recurrence Model* of participation in Forms, and so the regress develops. If f-things partake of parts of the Form F_1, then F_1 is f-similar to them. To explain this, Plato assumes that F_1 and all other f-things partake of a further Form F_2, and so on to infinity. However, Plato did not need to go this way, if only he had explained f-similarity here, too, as he had already explained it in the TBA. Recall that if, as per the TBA, Form F_1 had a form f_1 (an essence, in Aristotelian terms) that all f-entities would possess as well, whether they are sensible objects or Forms (just as all of F_1, F_2, and F_3 possess f_3 in the TBA), then F_1 would be *thereby* f-similar to all f-things (without partaking of any additional Form), in virtue of the fact that Form F_1, too, possesses form f_1, exactly in the way that F_3 was similar to F_1 and F_2 in the TBA – no regress ensues in this case. Plato however claims in the *Parmenides* that f-similars need to *partake* of the same Form F (rather than *possess* the same form f); therefore, he is thinking along the *Distributive Model* of participation.

For the sake of logical clarity, I want to distinguish between two ways of deriving the TMA Regress. First, given an object that partakes of a Form F and becomes f, since both the object and the Form are f, their similarity can be explained only if both of them partake of a Form F_2, which again is f, and so on to infinity. This is the first derivation of the TMA Regress. But this is not all that happens in the TMA. In the text, a contradiction lurks in the metaphysical background, too, from which a regress (and anything else) can logically follow. The contradiction derives, not by Plato's appeal to the *Distributive Model* (instead of the *Recurrence Model*) in the TMA, but from something more fundamental, namely his commitment to the *Contagion Principle*. The regress we just derived from Plato's use of the *Distributive Model* highlights a problem with the explanation of f-similarity only; the contradiction reveals a problem with the compatibility of the two different explanations of f-similarity according to the *Contagion Principle*. The problem is this: according to the *Contagion Principle*, when things partake of Form F, which is itself f, the things are each qualified as f, by each of them 'contracting' the Form's qualitative condition of f-ness. What generates the contradiction is that although each of the f-things aquires its f-ness from the qualitative condition of Form F, namely from the

Form's *f-ness*, and it *is therefore similar* to the Form, nevertheless, according to the *Contagion Principle*, the *f*-things *are not similar* to the Form. To become similar to Form F, all the *f*-things and Form F need to partake of a further Form F, namely F_2 and so on to infinity. (The *Contagion Principle* would not be able to explain the similarity between the Source F and the *f*'s, either, unless by positing further Sources F_2, F_3 ... .) From the contradiction, anything follows, including the regress.

The explanatory bankruptcy of the *Contagion Principle*, and the contradition, are clear if we focus on the source of *f-ness*. Things that partake of the source of *f-ness* acquire the *f-ness* of the source, becoming similar to it. But they can never become similar to the source of *f-ness*, because there is no further single source of *f-ness* from which they and the original source of *f-ness* could all acquire its same condition. Hence, the things that partake of the source of *f-ness* are and are not similar to it.

So the *Contagion Principle* undermines its very own assumptions; the ultimate problem lies in the fact that nothing in the *Contagion Principle* explains or justifies that the source of *f-ness* is *f*. So, since the *Contagion Principle*'s goal is to explain the *f-ness* of things, if it cannot explain the *f-ness* of the source, it cannot explain the *f-ness* of things. This is a deep-seated problem of the *Contagion Principle* that is revealed in the TMA, which is much more fundamental than a regress of Forms.

In thinking about the problem of the TMA for Plato's ontology, I assume the following theoretical points as fixed: first, Form *F* is *f*. The reason is that this is the core feature of the *Contagion Principle*: the source of *f-ness* must be *f*. Second, according to the *Contagion Principle*, *f*-things are *f*-similar to the source from which they 'contract' their *f-ness*; and so, in the theory of Forms, *f*-things are similar to the Form F they partake in to become *f*. Third, the *Contagion Principle* and respectively partaking in Form F account for both *f*-things being *f*, and *f*-things being *f*-similar to one another. As we saw, these three commitments give rise to infinite series of sources and of Forms. Concentrating now our attention on the Forms in the resulting series: all Forms in the regress are *f*, but numerically different from each other. Duplication is a problem: the TBA shows that there cannot be qualitatively identical Forms which are numerically different, which is also repeated in the *Parmenides* (131a8-b2): a Form cannot be separate from itself. In the TBA, Plato argued for the uniqueness of each type of Form; Plato cannot therefore, by his own principles, reify a Form F into an infinite series of *f*-Forms, which would also undermine the *One over Many Principle*.

Can Plato address the TMA challenge, if the option of reifying each *f*-Form into an infinite series of *f*-Forms is ruled out by the TBA and the *One over Many*

Principle? Gregory Vlastos's 1954 study is a milestone for modern debates around the TMA; he laid bare, in the premises of the argument, the principles around which discussions of the TMA and its possible solutions have subsequently centred. These are the *Self-Predication* (SP) and the *Non-Identity* (NI) premises. Both these premises are derived from the type of causal explanation provided by the *Contagion Principle*. Any *f*-thing contracts its *f-ness* from a distinct source of *f-ness* (NI), and the ultimate source of *f-ness* is itself *f* (SP). Yet, the model does not explain how an ultimate source of *f-ness* has become *f*. Plato undertakes to give such an explanation in the TMA about the *f-ness* of each Form F: applying the type of explanation offered by the *Contagion Principle* with consistency, for example if the Form of Heat is hot, it, too, is/has become hot by contagion, that is by partaking in a Form of Heat and so on to infinity. Therein lies the problem: if each ultimate source of *f-ness* has to become *f*, it cannot be the ultimate source of *f-ness*, on pain of contradiction.

Although a number of alternative solutions for avoiding the TMA Regress have been developed, what has not been appreciated so far is that Plato himself saves his theory from the seemingly fatal problems that TMA raises, by positing in the *Timaeus* that a Form F is *primitively f* – there is no further explanation of its *f-ness* because it does not become *f*. The Forms that make up the *paradeigma* in the *Timaeus* are not subject to becoming what they are (see 27d-28a); they simply are, have been and will remain the same (κατὰ ταὐτὰ ἔχον, 28a), which precludes a regress of Forms. This is a solution by *fiat*.[41]

I submit that the problem that Plato identifies at the root of the TMA Regress is a problem that plagues the *Contagion Principle*, which leaves open an explanatory lacuna with respect to the *f-ness* of the source. In a nutshell, the principle requires that *anything f* contracts its *f-ness* from the source of *f-ness*; but if the ultimate sourse of *f-ness becomes f* (by contracting its condition of *f-ness*, as *per* the *Contagion Principle*), it cannot be the ultimate source of *f-ness*; or else, if it does not become *f* by contracting *f-ness*, but it is primitively *f*, it is an exception to the very metaphysical rule that the *Contagion Principle* stands for. In the *Timaeus*, Plato opts for the primitiveness of the *f-ness* of Form F (the ultimate source of *f-ness*), taking the metaphysical stance that the Form does *not* become *f*.[42]

---

[41] As we will see in Section 4.4, there is an interesting parallel here to be drawn: in *Metaphysics* Z.6, Aristotle considers the possibility of a regress of essences within his system (different however from the TMA); and with the same move as Plato, blocks it by *fiat*: 'why should not some things be identified with their essence from the outset?' (Implicit answer: they should) (*Metaphysics* 1031b31). Plato's TMA regress is not the same regress as Aristotle's *Essence Regress*; but the TMA regress includes a regress of the essences of Forms – as each Form F participates in a further Form F to become *f*.

[42] The use of the verb 'become' in the above paragraphs is not intended to refer to a temporal dimension, which Forms clearly don't have, but only to constitutional complexity, such that something is made to be what it is by something else.

So far, we have discussed problems that are generated by Plato's distributive account of partaking in parts of a Form. Is there an alternative to the *Distributive Model*?

3.5 The *Likeness Regress*

Plato further develops an account of property qualification by imitation, which I call *Mimetic Model*; and uses it on some occasions as an alternative to the Anaxagorean *Distributive Model* (see for example *Parmenides* 132d, and *Republic* 597 c). On this alternative account, an object is qualified by a property by resembling the relevant Form, rather than by having a part of it within its constitution. The Forms are perfect paradigms of the properties they stand for, while objects in the world are imperfect copies of them.

Interestingly, Plato himself develops an argument *against* participation in Forms by imitation, but I argue that it is not a fair argument. It is a regress argument, immediately after the TMA in the *Parmenides*. I call it the *Likeness Regress*. Plato introduces the hypothesis that participation is by imitation, and shows that a regress of Forms of Likeness thereby develops:

> '[W]hat appears most likely to me is this: these forms are like patterns set in nature, and other things resemble [ἐοικέναι] them and are likenesses [ὁμοιώματα]; and this partaking of the forms is, for the other things, simply being modelled on them [εἰκασθῆναι αὐτοῖς].'
>
> 'If something resembles the form', he said, 'can that form not be like what has been modelled on it, to the extent that the thing has been made like it? Or is there any other way for something like to be like what it is not like it?' 'There is not.'
>
> 'And isn't there a compelling necessity for that which is like to partake of the same one form as what is like it?' 'There is.'
>
> 'But if like things are like by partaking of something, won't that be the form itself?' 'Undoubtedly.'
>
> 'Therefore nothing can be like the form, nor can the form be like anything else. Otherwise, alongside the form another form will always make its appearance, and if that form is like anything, yet another; and if the form proves to be like what partakes of it, a fresh form will never cease making its appearance.' 'This is very true.'
>
> 'So other things don't get a share of the forms by likeness'. (132d-133a)

The first few lines of the argument present two incompatible conditions for resembling a Form. First, Plato explains participation in a Form as resembling the Form:

> These forms are like patterns set in nature, and other things resemble them and are likenesses; and this partaking of the forms is, for the other things, simply being modelled on them. (132d1-4)

So, if Socrates partakes of the Form of Wisdom, then Socrates is like Wisdom. Plato adds that the Form, too, will be like the partaker that resembles it; likeness is a symmetrical relation:

> 'If something resembles the form', he said, 'can that form not be like what has been modelled on it, to the extent that the thing has been made like it? Or is there any other way for something like to be like what it is not like it?' 'There is not.' (132d)

This is exactly what we found in the TBA, where Forms F_1 and F_2 possess the form of Form F_3 and so they are like Form F_3, which is like them. This is the first criterion for being like a Form: that the partaker resembles the Form, and the Form resembles it. However, in the next sentence of the *Likeness Regress*, having established that a partaker of a Form will be like the Form, and the Form like the partaker, Plato states what I call the second criterion:

> 'And isn't there a compelling necessity for that which is like to partake of the same one form as what is like it?' 'There is.' (132d-e)

I argue that this second condition is directly incompatible with the first. According to the first condition, if an object partakes of a Form, it will resemble that Form, and the Form will resemble the partaker. According to the second condition, two things which are like each other necessarily partake of the same Form. Why? Logic tells us that a Form and its partaker need not both partake of a further Form in order to be like one another, because they are already like one another by the nature of the partaking relation between them. However, as we will see, Plato nevertheless uses both conditions in the argument to derive the *Likeness Regress*; this results in the breakdown of the logic of his argument, rendering it invalid, and hence, its conclusion unsound.

Let us go through the argument. What seems specific to this version of the theory of Forms is that, by its hypothesis, partaking of a Form F makes the partaker *f* by making it similar to Form F, with no need for both, partaker and Form, to partake of a further Form in order to be similar:[43]

> [W]hat appears most likely to me is this: these forms are like patterns set in nature, and other things resemble them and are likenesses; and this partaking of the forms is, for the other things, simply being modelled on them. (132d)

If a thing partakes of a Form, then the thing becomes similar to the Form. However, Plato continues:

---

[43] By contrast, in the TMA regress, similarity was conferred only when all similars partook of the same Form: 'I suppose you think each form is one on the following ground: whenever some number of things seem to you to be large, perhaps there seems to be some one character, the same as you look at them all, and from that you conclude that the large is one' (132a1-3).

'And isn't there a compelling necessity for that which is like to partake of the same one form as what is like it?' 'There is.' (132d-e)

This is alarming. Here Plato reverts to the standard explanation of similarity according to the theory of Forms: things are made similar by partaking of the same Form.[44] This claim is what generates the regress in the TMA,[45] by requiring a further Form for the similarity of each Form to its partaker; and this claim is, of course, consequential here too, in the *Likeness Regress*.

Although the statement that similars partake of the same Form sounds familiar to the reader who has just finished reading the TMA, on reflection, it is a shocking statement to read after Plato introduces participation in a Form as *similarity* to the Form, which does not require the partaker and the Form to partake of a further Form in order to be similar. That similarity requires participation in a further Form is a metaphysical 'rule' presented as necessary ('a compelling necessity') within the *Likeness Regress* argument; but there is nothing that makes this rule necessary within Plato's system. Interpreters of the *Likeness Regress* have not seen that Plato himself considers it possible to flout his own rule.[46] We have already seen Plato flout it, here by redefining participation as resemblance,[47] and in the TBA by explaining resemblance between a Form (F_3) and its partakers (F_1 and F_2) by the recurrence of the form of a Form (f_3). That Plato reverts to his rule and implicitly endorses the *Distributive Model* of participation, within the context of *Mimetic Model*, imposes a different logic to the *Likeness Regress* argument and gives rise to the regress.

Plato is careful to ascertain that if partakers are similar to the Form they partake of, the Form is also similar to them; so the Form cannot fail to be like its partaker (132d). He is now preparing us for the *Likeness Regress*: 'But if like things are like by partaking of something, won't that be the form itself?' 'Undoubtedly' (132e). The most straightforward reading that generates the *Likeness Regress* is the following, using only a single Form: of Likeness. Briefly put, a thing partakes of a Form, and so the thing and the Form become like each other; since the like things partake of the same Form (132d-e), both the things and the Form, which are like each other, partake of the Form of Likeness.

---

[44] 'Whenever some number of things seem to you to be large, perhaps there seems to be some one character, the same as you look at them all [...]', he said (132a).

[45] Since, as we just saw, partakers are similar to the Form they partake of, and further, similars partake of the same Form, it follows that the partakers and the (same) Form will also be similar between them, and so will partake of a further Form, ad infinitum.

[46] Thus for example Schofield writes: 'That is, the Form of Beauty in which the original Form of Beauty and beautiful things participate in virtue of the likeness in respect of beauty *must be another* Form of Beauty than the original' (1996: 62, my emphasis). Schofield does not see that likeness does not require this, even if Plato says it does.

[47] '[...] this partaking of the forms is, for the other things, simply being modelled on them' (132d).

However, it will always be the case that this (new) Form of Likeness will be 'like that which partakes of it', since it partakes of it, according to the new definition of partaking given here in terms of resemblance – by imitation (132d). So, each new Form of Likeness will be like its partakers, and hence, since likes partake of the same Form, a further Form of Likeness will emerge in which they all partake and so on ad infinitum.[48] The conclusion of the *Likeness Regress* argument develops this regress of Forms: 'if the form proves to be like what partakes of it, a fresh form will never cease emerging' (133a).

Participation by resemblance calls for the TBA's *Recurrence Model*. Plato's stance that his rule for similarity by participation in one and the same Form holds by necessity, is true only under specific conditions, and is false under other conditions. It is true under the *Distributive Model* of participation in Forms, but false under the *Recurrence Model*. On the *Distributive Model*, things are similar if they all partake of the same Form, because then the parts of the Form in each similar thing are similar because they are from the same source. On the *Recurrence Model*, things are similar if they possess the form of the Form in the TBA's language, because then it is the same form that qualifies each of all the similar things by recurring in them. So on the *Recurrence Model*, Plato's rule for similarity does not hold, even if declared to have 'compelling necessity' (*Parmenides* 132d9). Hence, the *Likeness Regress* develops based on the *Distributive Model*, even though one would have expected the *Recurrence Model* to be in play. The *Likeness Regress* is based on the *Distributive Model* because one of the premises of the argument is the rule for similarity which is true only on the *Distributive Model* and false on the *Recurrence Model*.[49] Generally, the *Distributive Model* assumes *similar parts* in the similar things; the *Recurrence Model* assumes *one and the same form* recurring in similar things.

Could Plato have avoided the *Likeness Regress* and provided a sound account of similarity here? Yes. We know that he entertains the possibility of universal properties recurring in things in more than one dialogue. In the TBA, the form f_3 of Form F_3 is possessed by F_3 as well as by F_1 and F_2. The recurrence of the form (f_3) of F_3 in F_1 and F_2, too, provides an explanation of the similarity between these three Forms. Such explanations of similarity, in terms of similar things

---

[48] An alternative way of deriving this regress would be with different types of Form than Likeness. Briefly, for example, if Socrates partakes of the Form of Virtue, they are both virtuous, and so they both partake of the Form of Virtue$_2$, and so resemble it, being virtuous, so they all partake of Virtue$_3$ and so on *ad infinitum*.

[49] The *Likeness Regress* conceived of on the *Distributive Model* can be visualised as follows: things are similar because they have qualitatively identical parts, for example two persons are dressed similarly when they are each wearing a red scarf. By contrast, on the *Recurrence Model*, they would share the very same recurring form, i.e. item of clothing, not similar ones.

having the *same* form (property) recurring in them, are metaphysically preferable to that of similar things possessing *similar* parts of a property, since this latter explanation is circular, explaining similarity in terms of similarity.

Why then did Plato *not* adopt recurring forms of Forms in his ontology as an explanation of similarity? The answer to this question can only be conjectural: if Plato introduced forms (essences) of Forms in his ontology, which recur in the many particulars, this would have raised fatal questions concerning the ontology of Forms. I submit that Plato must have been aware of the range and difficulties of such questions, and this must have dissuaded him from pursuing the idea further. The reason is that all the work of qualifying and making similar would have been done by the recurring essences of Forms, and so Forms themselves would not be needed in his ontology – if recurring essences of Forms can explain qualification and similarity of objects, why posit Forms at all? (Aristotle on the other hand, as we will see in Section 4, developed an ontology of recurring universals only, and had no place or need for any Forms in the ontology.)

Furthermore, if a Form had an essence, the Form would be 'divided' into subject and essence – with the essence belonging to the Form as its subject (Form F is *f*). This would be a fundamental problem for Plato, who holds that Forms are *kath' hauto f* (e.g. *Phaedo* 78d5). Plato does not explain anywhere precisely what being *kath' hauto f* is, but he applies this notion to Forms, which is the best directive for us as to how to understand this notion, which is unfamiliar to contemporary philosophy. I understand being *kath' hauto f* as the denial of what we call now (after Aristotle) essential predication; the requirement is that the ultimate subject in a *kath' hauto f* entity is *f-ness* itself; so the Form of Justice, in itself, *is* Justice. If however *f-ness* is essentially predicated of a subject, it follows that the subject is not *kath' hauto f*. Plato could not accept this, for his Forms, which he claims are *kath' hauto f*.

3.6 Partless Complexity

There are certain moments in the history of philosophy when a milestone is marked by the simple fact that a particular thought is formulated. This is the case when Plato in the *Theaetetus* conceives the idea that a form (a property) can unify the parts of a composite into a partless whole. This is a thought that has stood the test of time in the history of philosophy, having been developed in various theories of metaphysical *emergence*. It is a thought that gives us a further insight into Plato's theory of properties, even if Plato himself did not develop it further.

Plato writes in the *Theaetetus* that a composite entity can be unified into a single *partless* whole by its form (its essence, in Aristotelian terms). He explains thus:

> 'Let the complex be a single form [ἰδέα] resulting from the combination of the several elements when they fit together; and let this hold both of language and of things in general.' 'Yes, certainly.' 'Then it must have no parts.' 'Why is that, now?' 'Because when a thing has parts, the whole is necessarily all the parts.' (204a)[50]

This is Plato's conceptual breakthrough: the thought that a property, in some cases and under certain conditions, unites a composite of interrelated parts into a partless whole. Plato's examples of composites are syllables (e.g. 'SO') and numbers (e.g. 6; see 204c and 205a-b), but in the passage quoted in this section he generalises the position. For Plato, the parts of an entity determine its number (204e), so if the entity is partless, it is altogether one; and if it has any parts, it is many – a point that will shape Aristotle's thinking in the *Categories*, as I will argue in Section 4.

The attractiveness of Plato's idea is that it enables us to understand how a complex can be a *partless* whole. The partless whole results from different elements, which is why it is complex. The complexity deriving from its different elements might of be of any number of types. The whole could be complex in the sense of being qualitatively diverse, where the qualities are not parts of the whole, but are nevertheless different from one another. (Or it could be that the elements from which the whole was generated have now become potential parts of the whole, as in Aristotle's mixtures (e.g. seawater), where the elements survive in potentiality in the whole, but not as parts of it.[51])

Plato's thought is philosophically momentous, and its reverberations are strongly felt even in today's metaphysics. I contend in Section 4 that Aristotle appropriated it centrally into his own metaphysics, making it the ground of his theory that a substance is unified by its substantial form.[52]

3.7 Conclusion

Plato addresses centrally in his metaphysics the problems of qualification and qualitive similarity between things, by developing an ontology of Forms, which stand for properties; things in the world become qualified with these properties

---

[50] I have offered an analysis of what I call the *Dilemma of Composition* in Marmodoro (2021, section 5.2).

[51] See *Generation and Corruption* 10.1.

[52] Substances have functional 'parts', but these 'parts' are defined by, and are dependent on, the unifying substantial form (see *Metaphysics* 1035b).

by partaking in the respective Forms. I showed that the attractiveness of Plato's theory of Forms as an explanation of qualification and similarity lies in its conformity with the *Contagion Principle*, which was a traditional way at the time of thinking about qualification and similarity but which, I argued, brought severe problems to Plato's theory.

I showed that Plato brought into play in his metaphysics three conceptions of partaking in Forms, where a thing partakes by possessing a part of a Form, or by similarity with the Form, or by possessing the form (essence) of a Form. The first is the *Distributive Model*, by which a Form is distributed to many things that partake in it by possessing parts of the Form; the second is the *Mimetic Model*, by which things that partake in a Form resemble the Form; and the third is the *Recurrence Model*, by which things resemble a Form by possessing the form of the Form.

Had the *Mimetic Model* been fully articulated by Plato, it might have replaced the *Contagion Principle* in the explanation of qualification and similarity, by resemblance. However, as Plato formulated it, the *Mimetic Model* does not explain how resemblance occurs; thus it has remained uninfluential in the history of metaphysics. The *Recurrence Model* instead succeeds the *Contagion Principle* as an explanation of qualification and similarity; Plato discovered it but never developed it or fully endorsed it in his system; it is Aristotle who will make it a central piece of own theory of properties. The *Recurrence Model* is not without its own difficulties; it challenges the oneness of each Form, by 'dividing' the Form into subject and essence. While this does not surface in Plato's metaphysics as a problem, it does surface subsequently in Aristotle's *Essence Regress*, as we shall see in Section 4.

I concluded this section by mentioning possibly the most long-lasting Platonic contribution to the metaphysics of properties, namely that a property can unite the parts of a complex into a partless whole. I will show in the next section how this Platonic metaphysical innovation was picked up and adopted by Aristotle.

4 Aristotle's Forms

It is well known that Aristotle conceives of properties as universals, which are 'in' the world as 'instantiated' in objects. The difficulty is how to understand what it is for a universal to be instantiated, and even multiply instantiated, that is: recur whole in multiple locations at once. According to the mainstream view, in the scholarly literature and also in ongoing discussions of Aristotle's theory in current metaphysics, instantiation is one metaphysical phenomenon. My claim (for which I will argue in Sections 4.2 and 4.3) is that Aristotle distinguishes (at least implicitly) two different metaphysical phenomena, for which he provides different explanations: instantiation as the phenomenon by which properties qualify objects, and instantiation as the phenomenon by which properties occur in the world as actual. Confusedly the two phenomena are referred to with the same term in the literature. For clarity, in what follows I will reserve the term instantiation for the first phenomenon only.

A further consideration to make before going forward is that there are two pillars on which a fair understanding of Aristotle's metaphysics has to lean: first, the centrality in his thinking of the *unity* and the *uniqueness* of a substance, both of which are for him types of *oneness*. Second, his philosophical dependencies on Plato: I show that Aristotle advances in several novel ways positions that Plato was the first to introduce; we can understand Aristotle's theory in full only if we take this into consideration. In very general terms, arguably the most important stance in relation to which Aristotle's metaphysics depends on Plato's is that *a property can unify the parts of a whole into a partless whole* (recall Plato's *Theaetetus* 204–205, here discussed in Section 3.6). We will see that Aristotle adopts this stance from the start, in the *Categories*. We will also see that Aristotle will justifiably feel he has much more to explain and therefore more to supply than what Plato did in the *Theaetetus*, if he is to claim, as he does, that a property (the substantial form) unifies the components of a substance into a single entity. I will show that there are two metaphysical challenges that Aristotle faces. One is similar to Plato's challenge in the *Theaetetus*; Aristotle, too, needs to show that the components of substance are unified into a single partless whole (which Aristotle assumed substances to be in the *Categories*, and, with more difficulties to face, in his *Metaphysics*). The second metaphysical challenge is more complex: Aristotle needs to argue that the subject–essence division within a substance does not undermine the oneness of the substance. The origins of this second challenge are to be traced back to Plato's TBA, where the division of (Plato's) substances (the Forms) into subject and essence first appears. Aristotle raises difficulties related to the subject–essence division within a substance, as we will see in the analysis of *Metaphysics* Z.3 (here in Section 4.3), and of his *Essence Regress* in Z.6. (here in Section 4.4). However, Aristotle's position on this issue is fundamentally different from Plato's, and most importantly, he has a solution, which he starts developing from the *Categories* onwards, by building each substance 'around' its essence (e.g. Socrates as a qualified human being). This is, I will argue, his solution to the problem of the subject–essence division within a substance, which also shows the substance to be *kath' hauto* its essence.

4.1 Properties Are Not Parts of Substances

In his *Categories*, Aristotle provides the first systematic classification of properties in the history of metaphysics. His aim is to classify all types of properties that describe what and how things are. The result is not a list of all there is, but a schema, where all there is can be classified. The properties classified in this metaphysical schema serve as building blocks of Aristotle's substances, for example Socrates, this tree or that stone. Aristotle's ontology however differs profoundly from those we have already encountered of Anaxagoras and Plato: properties are not fundamental for Aristotle, in the sense in which they are for his predecessors. In the *Categories* he writes:

> Thus all the things [namely, properties] are either said of the primary sub-stances [e.g. Socrates] as subjects or in them as subjects. So if the primary substances did not exist, it would be impossible for any of the other things [properties in the categorial scheme, e.g. being pale] to exist. (2b4-6)

Here Aristotle claims that properties exist in the world only as belonging to substances, and he distinguishes between two ways in which they belong: properties are 'said of' or 'in' substances.[53] The point of paramount importance for our purposes here is that for Aristotle all properties, those 'said of' and those 'in' a substance, are said of it and are in it *as their subject*.[54] Before unpacking the significance of this statement, I want to highlight that he also explicitly claims:

> By 'in a subject' I mean what is in something, *not as a part*, and cannot exist separately from what it is in. (1a24-25, my emphasis)

On my reading of these lines, for Aristotle properties are 'in' substances as their building blocks; but his position is very different from that of Anaxagoras and

---

[53] Aristotle distinguishes between the way essences are predicated of substances and the way accidents are predicated of them in terms of two forms of predication: essences are 'said of' substances, while accidents are 'in' substances. This is to say that essences are in substances in a way different from that in which accidents are in them. In the *Categories*, Aristotle does not explain this difference, for which we will need to wait until the *Metaphysics*. This difference is not of concern to us here for our present purposes.

[54] Mann (2000) contrasts Anaxagoras's, Plato's and Aristotle's ontologies, attributing to Aristotle 'the discovery of things', by which Mann means:

> 'Accordingly, the discovery of things amounts to the discovery . . . that all the entities need to be divided into particular objects on the one hand, and whatever belongs to those objects on the other (including whatever kinds those objects fall under, in other words, their species and genera). To this Aristotle adds the further claim that the objects, the *bona fide* things, [that is, the particular objects] are the most fundamental entities' (2000: 10–11).

This section aims to explain, metaphysically, what 'things' are for Aristotle and what it is for properties to 'belong' to things, which is a task that Mann has left undone.

Plato, who thought, as we saw, that parts of properties are parts of objects. Aristotle explicitly rejects that position: the properties of the substance are not 'in' it *as parts*. However, he neither explains nor justifies this statement in the *Categories*. I submit that his stance here must be underpinned by Plato's stance in the *Theaetetus*, that the number of a thing is the number of its parts (204e1-2). Thus, a thing with parts is many, not one; and a thing that is one is partless. If Aristotle follows Plato in thinking that a number of a thing is the number of its parts, the properties of a substance cannot be parts of the substance, because each substance is numerically one, as Aristotle explicitly assumes in the *Categories*. On this line of thinking we can make very good sense of the stance he takes, and leaves unjustified, that properties are not parts of substances: they cannot be, if the substance is numerically one (a problem that neither Anaxagoras or Plato were concerned about). Thus, if the properties of a substance are 'in' it, they need to be 'in' it in a way that does not undermine the oneness of the substance. Hovever, neither Aristotle in the *Categories* nor Plato in the *Theaetetus* gives an account of *how* this is achieved metaphysically. I contend that there is a way according to Aristotle for components not to be parts of the whole they are in, if when in the whole, their individuality is somehow 'undermined', so that they are in the whole but not as discrete entities/parts in it. Aristotle talks about his position only in the briefest of terms, later in the *Metaphysics*; but in the *Categories* we find an initial clue, where he assumes that properties in the world are either 'said of' or 'in' a subject. What is the significance of their being said of or in *a subject*?

Importantly, Aristotle tells us that the definition of, for example, 'whiteness', which is predicated truly of the property 'whiteness' in the categorial scheme, is *not* predicated of the subject that whiteness qualifies, for example a body – so, what is white is not whiteness. He writes in the *Categories*:

> In some cases there is nothing to prevent the name from being predicated of the subject, but it is impossible for the definition to be predicated. For example, white, which is in a subject (the body), is predicated of the subject; for a body is called white. But the definition of white will never be predicated of the body. (2a29-34)[55]

On my reading, Aristotle is indicating here when a property *qualifies* a substance, it does not do so by being present in the substance: for example, 'whiteness' as a qualification of a body is not the presence of 'whiteness' in a body; it is, rather, the body's being white; the body is not whiteness, but it is

---

[55] Of course, this does not apply to substantial forms, for example being human. Aristotle is clear that the above applies only to the properties from the non-substance categories, namely only to things which are *in a subject*. For substantial forms, which are the essences of substances, their definition is *said of* the substances. So, substances are what their essences are, for example 'human', for Socrates; and properties qualify what substances are, such as it is the human that is wise.

white. How can this be explained metaphysically? I understand Aristotle's position as follows: a property's instantiation in a substance is a type of 'transformation' of the universal,[56] which of course one cannot perceive, but only conceive. It is a transformation of the property, *from being an uninstantiated abstract entity*, as the property is defined, for example as 'whiteness', *to being the qualification of a particular concrete subject*, such as a white body.

Before we come to address what type of transformation this is, I want to note that here Aristotle is taking forward one of Plato's conclusions in the TBA (here discussed in Section 3.3). We saw that in the TBA, Plato claims that Forms F_1 and F_2, which are posited initially *per hypothesis* as two Forms of Bed, are not Forms, only F_3 is. However, Plato does not offer a metaphysical explanation of this claim; why are F_1 and F_2 not Forms? I have argued that they are not Forms, because the numerical difference between F_1 and F_2, and their numerical difference from F_3 requires F_1 and F_2 to be ontologically different from (in Plato's example) 'what it is to be bed'. I contend that Aristotle's answer would be the same, and even more general, for all properties: the instances of a property differ from the property as such (as given in its definition), by whatever differentiates the instances between them, for example as F_1 and F_2. (F_1 and F_2 cannot both be exactly 'what it is to be bed', but also numerically different between them.) Aristotle will develop further this account in the *Metaphysics*.

At this point, a clarification is in order, concerning the status of Aristotle's properties/forms, which 'enter' the constitution of substances. For Aristotle, properties exist only 'in' substances, not on their own, by themselves (e.g. in the way that Forms exist on their own in Plato's ontology). So strictly speaking, properties can never 'enter' or be 'extracted from' the substance they qualify: they are always in substances; and of course properties do not undergo any type of ordinary change when they are subject to a 'transformation' when instantiated. This language, albeit only figuratively, helps us understand a crucial point in Aristotle's metaphysics of properties: properties are 'extracted from' substances *by abstraction* – properties 'in' a substance can be *abstracted from it*. With this *proviso*, what I have tried to describe earlier in this section is that a property as an abstracted entity is metaphysically different from a property component of a substance instantiated in it.[57] In general, abstraction is a mental operation by which one can strip away all that is different between similar things,

---

[56] I use the expression 'transformation' here for lack of a more appropriate term; I do not mean to say that universals undergo any kind of ordinary change when instantiated. More on this to follow.

[57] I see this as a direct application of Aristotle's *Homonymy Principle*, where what belongs to a substance is different from what can be severed from the substance (see Section 4.7).

until what they have in common (in our case the property F) is individuated as an abstract entity that can be abstracted from many objects (whiteness from white roses, white snow, white bears, etc.). I submit that in Aristotle's metaphysics, abstraction is the key to understanding qualification, similarity and the recurrence of properties. (Importantly, even if abstraction is a mental operation, an abstracted universal is *not* a mental entity whose existence depends on the existence of minds, any more than the undetached components of a substance, for example the undetached slices of a cake, are mental entities, because they are individuated by abstraction.)

4.2 Property Instantiation

In very general terms, for the ancient philosophers whom we are considering, a property qualifies a substance by being 'in' it, that is by being in some way included in the constitution of the substance. On the *Distributive Model*, such inclusion is, at least intuitively, straightforward to understand: a part of the property comes to be a part of the object, and property and object overlap constitutionally. But we saw Aristotle has reasons to reject this model, where properties are present as such in objects. How is a property in an object according to the alternative *Recurrence Model*? Much philosophical work is still to be done, not only to understand how Aristotle conceives of the problem and which solutions he has to offer but also more generally in metaphysics, to understand the value and perhaps the limits of the *Recurrence Model* as an alternative to the *Distributive Model*.

We saw that for Plato, in the TBA, the Forms could *per hypothesis* multiply themselves and thus recur only at the cost of losing their status as Forms, becoming constitutionally different. The TBA reveals to us Plato's insight (which he however does not pursue) that instantiation makes a difference to the constitution of the instantiated property – instantiation is not a 'free lunch', metaphysically. The thrust of my argument here is that Aristotle makes Plato's insight the core of his theory of instantiation, by offering an account of how a property is instantiated 'in' a substance, not by its presence in the substance, but *by becoming a qualification* of it. As already anticipated in Section 4.1, for Aristotle, a universal *qua* instantiated in an object, as a property component of a substance (e.g. Socrates is wise), is metaphysically different from the universal *qua* abstracted from the object, as an abstract entity (e.g. wisdom). In what way different?

Aristotle posits that the property *as instantiated* in a substance is not individuated *as the property as such*, as a discrete existence within the substance. A property as such is individuated by its definition, for example 'whiteness' is defined as a colour of certain specifications. If the property is individuated in a substance as such, as a discrete component with its own definition, it would undermine the oneness of the substance. (Recall Plato's position that the number of a thing is the number of its parts.) For Aristotle, the first step for including a property 'in' a substance without undermining the oneness of the substance is to deprive the property of its own individuation criterion, given by its definition. I take Aristotle to be doing just this when he writes that when 'a body is called white ... the definition of white will never be predicated of the body' (*Categories* 2a27 ff.). The *only* definition predicated of a substance, and which provides the individuation criterion for the substance, is the definition of the substantial form:

> It is clear from what has been said that if something is said of a subject, both its name and its definition are necessarily predicated of the subject. For example, 'man' is said of a subject, the individual man, and the name is of course predicated (since you will be predicating man of the individual man), and also the definition of man will be predicated of the individual man (since the individual man is also a man). (2a19-25)

We learned in the *Categories* that the definition of a property is not predicated of the substance which the property qualifies – Socrates is not wisdom but wise, and a body is not whiteness but white. On my understanding, this means that the property that qualifies a substance is deprived of its own, independent individuation principle, so it is not present in the subtance as a (self-standing) part of the substance. So, for now, Aristotle has excised the individuation criteria (i.e. the definitions) of each of the properties that qualify the substance; we shall see immediately following that he takes a further step – of supplying these properties with a new individuation criterion, the individuation criterion of the substance itself (through the substance's definition).

In the *Metaphysics*, Aristotle makes a complementary move, which, on my reading, supplies the properties that qualify a substance with a new individuation criterion, *qua qualifications* of the substance. In the context of explaining the existential primacy of substance, Aristotle says that by contrast to substance, 'none of the other categories [of properties] can exist separately' (1028a33); and then he introduces what I call the *Embedding Principle* (but he does not explain what this principle does, other than show the *primacy of the definition* of substance). The *Embedding Principle* is expressed by Aristotle as follows:

> And in formula also this [i.e. substance] is primary; for in the formula of each term [i.e. of a property of the substance] the formula of its substance must be present. (1028a35)

According to the *Embedding Principle*, the definition of a substance in which a property is instantiated 'enters' the definition of the instantiated property. I submit that embedding the definition of a substance into the definitions of its property components imports the individuation criterion of the type of substance it is, into the definition of the components. So, for instance, the definition of a wall is embedded into the definition of the white of the wall. The result is that the embedded definition of the substance gives the property its individuation criterion; for example, whiteness is now individuated through the individuation criterion of the wall as 'white wall' rather than as compresent whiteness+wall.

What is the metaphysical significance of this principle? This principle is at the core of Aristotle's system, playing a fundamental role not only in his account of the instantiation of properties but also in the account of the unity of substance, as we will see. The move Aristotle makes in the *Metaphysics* finally explains his claim in the *Categories* that the properties of a substance are not parts of it – they are not parts, because they are not individuated as the properties they are (as such, and thus as discrete); rather, they have become qualifications of the substance; they qualify *it*. Furthermore, this metaphysical move of 'transforming' universal properties into qualifications of the substance also delivers the oneness of the substance as a unified single kind, with a unified single defiition (e.g. being a human being), as opposed to being a bundle of properties (being mortal, being rational, being pale etc.).

In the *Metaphysics*, Aristotle succinctly raises the following problem about the oneness of the definition of a substance:

> I mean this problem: – wherein consists the unity of that, the formula of which we call a definition, as for instance in the case of man: two-footed animal; for let this be the formula of man. Why, then, is this one, and not many, viz. animal *and* two-footed? For in the case of 'man' and 'white' there is a *plurality* when one term *does not belong* to the other, but a *unity* when *it does belong* and the subject, man, has a certain attribute [i.e. qualification]; for then a *unity* is produced and we have the 'white man'. (1037b11-17, my emphasis)

I read this text as confirming the analysis I offered earlier in this section. In the present passage, Aristotle says that individual universal properties, where the one does not qualify the other, are many (here, two: 'man' and 'white'); but when the one qualifies the other, they are one, as in the case of 'white man'. This is explicit indication that Aristotle holds that qualification unifies (namely, when a property becomes the qualification of a substance, the outcome is one qualified substance, rather than the collection (as it were) of a compresent property and substance); thus, in the definition of a substance, the genus is the subject of the *differentia*: man is a rational animal. The oneness of a substance and its qualification shows the unity of the qualified substance, not its particularity.

On my understanding, Aristotle follows his generally empiricist approach for accounting for the particularity of a substance, which is established by the properties that qualify *it*.[58] It is fair to say that this way of establishing particularity will not address problems that have been raised in non-empiricist contexts in later periods of the history of philosophy, for example how to distinguish between individuals who recur in infinitely repeated Stoic conflagrations,[59] or between Max Black's Two Spheres (1952). An empiricist like Aristotle would have remained unruffled, simply because such problems of identification do not occur within the world of experience.

4.3 The Occurrence of Properties in the World

We saw that for Aristotle a property that is instantiated in a substance is deprived of its definition (i.e. its individuation criterion as a property), and it is supplied with the definition of the substance (i.e. the individuation criterion of the substance), so that the property is now individuated as a qualification of the substance, rather than as a property/entity in its own right. This is Aristotle's solution to the problem of how properties are instantiated in substances: by becoming their qualifications. There is however a further problem concerning properties that Aristotle addresses – a problem which did not arise for Anaxagoras because for him properties are physical entities 'directly' in the world. For Plato, for most of his philosophical trajectory, properties are transcendent, and thus not in the physical world; however, Plato is the first, in the *Timaeus* (as we will see later in this section), to show awareness of the question of how properties are *in nature*; and he attempts a solution via the so-called Receptacle. Aristotle, I contend, following the later Plato, wants to provide a metaphysical explanation for the fact that properties are occurent in nature, 'actual', we might say.[60] He does not treat this as a brute fact, as Anaxagoras does, but he provides an account of it in *Metaphysics* Z.3.

Aristotle sees clearly that the occurrence of properties *as actual, occurring in the world* is a different phenomenon from the instantiation of properties in substances *as the qualifications of substances*, as I show following. My aim here is to show how they are different, and to reconstruct how Aristotle explains each. While in Section 4.2 we were concerned with instantiation as qualification, here we are concerned with occurrence.

---

[58] On this point, see Marmodoro (2022a).

[59] Where the physical world recurs exactly the same infinitely many times in its history.

[60] Their being *actual* by occurring in nature is metaphysically different from their being *actualities* as forms, or their being *actualised*, according to Aristotle's account of potentiality and actuality.

Aristotle addresses the occurrence of properties in *Metaphysics* Z.3, where he introduces what we would call a thought experiment, which I call his *Stripping Away Argument*.[61] I supply here the section of Aristotle's text that will be central to our discussion:

> When all else is taken away [from a body] evidently *nothing but matter remains*. For of the other elements some are affections, products, and capacities of bodies, while length, breadth, and depth are quantities and not substances. For a quantity is not a substance; but the substance is rather that to which these belong primarily. But when length and breadth and depth are taken away, we see nothing left except that which is bounded by these whatever it be; so that to those who consider the question thus matter alone must seem to be a substance. By matter I mean that which in itself is neither a particular thing nor of a certain quantity nor assigned to any other of the categories by which being is determined. For there is something of which each of these is predicated, so that *its being* is different from that of each of the predicates; for the predicates other than substance are predicated of substance, while substance is predicated of matter. Therefore the ultimate substratum is of itself neither a particular thing nor of a particular quantity nor otherwise positively characterized; nor yet negatively, for negations also will belong to it only by accident. (1029a11-26)

Aristotle starts his thought experiment with a qualified substance and proceeds to abstract its qualities away from it. The substance's qualities that Aristotle individuates here by abstraction are the beings – the forms – that he had reified and classified in the *Categories'* scheme. What has exercised all readers of *Metaphysics* Z.3 is that at the end of his thought experiment, after abstracting away all the qualifications of a substance, Aristotle finds that 'something' of the substance is still 'left behind': surprisingly, it has no being of any categorial kind, not even the being of their negations (e.g. being 'not red'). Aristotle gives a *prima facie* 'baffling' description of his finding, here extracted from the passage just quoted:

> For there is something of which each of these is predicated, so that its being is different from that of each of the predicates; for the predicates other than substance are predicated of substance, while substance is predicated of

---

[61] Interpreters have disagreed since antiquity on how to read *Metaphysics* Z.3; it is impossible within the scope of this Element to pay justice to all existing lines of interpretation. Before articulating my own, it will be helpful to recall the mainstream view in the scholarly literature, and even in ongoing discussions of Aristotle's theory in current metaphysics: it is thought that the 'something more' in a substance is some sort of particular entity, namely matter (or even 'prime' matter, or a bare particular, according to some), understood as what particularises properties in substances by entering into some sort of relation with them. At the other end of the spectrum, as it were, other scholars think that nothing is left after abstraction; for instance, Schofield (1972) says: 'My own inclination is to take the clause "unless ... " to be an inept gloss' (1972: 99).

matter. *Therefore the ultimate substratum is of itself neither a particular thing nor of a particular quantity nor otherwise positively characterized; nor yet negatively,* for negations also will belong to it only by accident. (1029a22-26, my emphasis)

A puzzle emerges here: how can there be something whose *being is not any of the kinds of being* in the ontology of being? Aristotle does not answer in *Metaphysics* Z.3 this and similar questions that arise there. What 'is left' after abstraction is not a categorial property, nor body, nor the substantial form of the substance of which all the properties are predicated. Nevertheless, enigmatically, what 'is left' is something that 'has being'.

I suggest that, if it is not the subject (i.e. the substantial form), nor its properties, all of which have been abstracted away from the substance, the only thing that could be left after all these have been astracted away is what made it possible for all these properties to occur in nature, as actual properties in the world. What could that be?

Aristotle calls what is left 'matter' (ὕλη, 1029a11), which does not help us, since the only type of matter we are acquainted with, so far, in his system is physical body, and 'what is left', is not physical body. He (under-)describes 'what is left' as something 'which is bounded by these [properties] whatever it be' (1029a19). He then adds something further about the metaphysical role this matter plays: it is the 'ultimate substratum' or subject; the 'substance [i.e. the substantial form, and all the qualities predicated of it] *is predicated of* matter' (1029a23-24).

This is bewildering, since we know, and Aristotle states here again, that the subject of the properties of the substance is the substantial form. This is a metaphysical position that has not changed since the *Categories*, where Aristotle first described it. However, here, Aristotle seemingly – and alarmingly! – posits *two* subjects in a substance:

for the predicates other than substance are predicated of substance, while substance is predicated of matter. (1029a23-24)

If we read these lines at face value, Aristotle would be claiming that one of the subjects is the essence of the substance (its substantial form), while the second subject is something propertyless, not particular, not individual and not separate. Is he truly committing to the position that there are two subjects in each substance? This cannot be. Rather, I contend, he is distinguishing between two different phenomena he wants to explain in his metaphysics: that properties *qualify* substances and that properties *occur* in nature. Aristotle speaks as if there were two subjects, to indicate – for lack of a more precise and articulate philosophical jargon – that there are two different metaphysical phenomena:

a property qualifies a substance and it occurs in nature. (More on Aristotle's language later in this section.)

On the interpretation I offered in Section 4.2, for Aristotle a property is instantiated when it becomes a *qualification* of an object, or, if it is a substantial form, when it is *qualified* by properties. Becoming a qualification and becoming qualified are metaphysically complex processes, as we have seen, and they describe what the instantiation of properties is metaphysically. Aristotle holds this view consistently throughout his earlier and later writings, the *Categories* and the *Metaphysics*. What more is needed to round off his metaphysics of properties and substances? Or put differently, what does the matter of *Metaphysics* Z.3 'do' for a substance?

The interpretative key, I believe, is to be found by examining *Metaphysics* Z.3 vis-à-vis Plato's *Timaeus*. I contend that in *Metaphysics* Z.3 Aristotle is responding and building on Plato's *Timaeus*, in ways that have not been yet discussed in the relevant literature. In a nutshell, before offering my full argument, in the *Timaeus* (49–51) Plato posits a Receptacle, which receives 'copies'[62] of the Forms (the properties of things in the world), and which *qua* Space gives each bundle of copies of the Forms a unique location.[63] So things are created in the Receptacle out of bundles of copies of the Forms (but their properties do not qualify the Receptacle – we will return to this point in what follows). I take Plato's account of the Receptacle in the *Timaeus* to be a first metaphysical explanation of what it is for a property (here, a copy of a Form) to be actual or occurrent in the physical world, on which Aristotle will build in *Metaphysics* Z.3. Properties in Aristotle's system occur in propertyless matter, as they occur in the propertyless Receptacle in Plato's system. (Aristotle in a sense simplifies Plato's account, focusing only on what it is for a property to be actual, and nothing else; while Plato gives the Receptacle also the job of giving properties a unique spatial location.)[64]

Aristotle claims that matter as the ultimate subject is *propertyless*. In the *Timaeus*, Plato holds that the Receptacle receives copies of the Forms in it,

---

[62] Plato says about the Receptacle, 'the figures that enter [it] and depart [it] are copies of those that are always existent', that is of the Forms (*Timaeus* 50c; see also 50a and 50b). We will not however enter here in a discussion of why Plato speaks of copies of the Forms.

[63] Plato describes our cognitive access to the Receptacle in the *Timaeus* as follows: 'It is apprehended by a kind of bastard reasoning that does not involve sense pereception, and it is hardly even an object of conviction. We look at it as in a dream when we say that everything that exists must of necessity be somewhere and in a place and occupying some space, and that that which doesn't exist somewhere, whether on earth or in heaven, does not exist at all' (52b).

[64] Plato writes: '[...] everything that exists must of necessity be somewhere and in a place and occupying some space, and that that which doesn't exist somewhere, whether on earth or in heaven, does not exist at all' (*Timaeus* 52b). The Receptacle is what makes it possible for things (intended generically as including properties too) to be in space.

giving rise to the world of Becoming, where things are generated, changed and destroyed:

> Now the same account, in fact, holds also for that nature which receives all the bodies. We must always refer to it by the same term; for it does not depart from its own character in any way. Not only does it always receive all things, *it has never in any way whatever taken on any characteristic similar to any of the things that enter it.* Its nature is to be available for anything to make its impression upon, and it is modified, shaped and reshaped by the things that enter it. These are the things that *make it appear* [φαίνεται] different at different times. The things that enter and leave it are imitations of those things that always are, imprinted after their likeness in a marvellous way that is difficult to describe. (50b-c)

The properties that occur in the Receptacle do not however qualify the Receptacle, but make it only *appear* like themselves, for example fiery. The Receptacle does not have any of the properties that it receives in it, so that its own nature does not interfere with the natures that occupy it:

> We also must understand that if the imprints are to be varied, with all the varieties there to see, this thing upon which the imprints are to be formed could not be well prepared for that role it it were not *itself devoid of any those characters that it is to receive from elsewhere.* (50d, my emphasis)

What is important for present purposes is that the Receptacle is nevertheless described by Plato as having its *own nature*, from which it never departs. Importantly, the nature of the Receptacle is a type of being which does not correspond to any type of being that the Forms stand for. This indicates that Plato's ontology is not exhausted by the Forms of being; there is more in the cosmos than the Forms. We have encountered this in Aristotle's account in *Metaphysics* Z.3, too; we can return now to the issue and understand in more depth how Aristotle conceives of his *ultimate matter*.

The 'being' of the ultimate propertyless matter in *Metaphysics* Z.3 is *prima facie* perplexing; but we now see that it is a development of an originally Platonic idea. Like Plato's Receptacle, Aristotle's ultimate matter is not characterised by any of the forms of being, which Aristotle classifies in the *Categories*. It is clearly not the matter of physical things, namely physical body, such as marble, flesh and bones. However, again like Plato's Receptacle, Aristotle's matter in *Metaphysics* Z.3 does have being. My interpretative proposal is as follows: there are some properties, I submit, for example 'being a substance', which do not describe the kind something is. Just as there is no quality of 'being a substance' in the categorial scheme, so there is no quality of 'being en-mattered' in the categorial scheme, either. Such is Aristotle's claim about the *being* of propertyless matter in

Metaphysics Z.3 – we can call it a meta-categorial being.[65] I understand the nature of Plato's Receptacle along the same lines; it has being that is not captured by any of the Forms of being.

Returning now to what metaphysical function the Receptacle serves for in Plato's system, Aristotle insightfully describes the Receptacle as space, which serves metaphysically as the matter of things:

> This is why Plato in the *Timaeus* says that matter and space [τὴν χώραν] are the same; for the 'participant' [μεταληπτικὸν][66] and space are identical. (*Physics*, 209b11-12)

This is right. Plato allots two distinct metaphysical functions to the Receptacle: it *receives* the copies of the Forms in it, and it *particularises* these copies (properties) through their location in the Receptacle as Space (Place). I will argue that Aristotle, in his account in *Metaphysics* Z.3, separates these two metaphysical functions and focuses on the first to explain how properties become *actual* in nature. For Plato, a copy of a Form occurs in a location in space, and is thereby particularised. Plato believes that 'everything that exists must of necessity be somewhere and in a place and occupying some space' (52b). By contrast to Plato's Receptacle, Aristotle's ultimate matter does not particularise the forms it receives, because there is nothing in ultimate matter's nature that would enable it to serve this metaphysical role. (Recall that Aristotle claims explicitly that his ultimate matter is not a particular thing (1029a24).)

What, then, is its metaphysical role? The most important clue we have to reconstruct Aristotle's view is that ultimate matter has no categorial being (but only meta-categorial being); therefore, it is *no addition* to the ontology of a substance. It does not attribute any categorial being to the substance; it does not particularise the properties of the substance; it does not even serve as the subject of the properties of the substance, becoming qualified by them (as I argue, immediately below in this section).[67] I submit that ultimate matter does one thing only, metaphysically: it marks out the properties that are actual, that is that occur in the cosmos, and nothing else.

In arguing for my interpretation that ultimate matter does not serve as the subject of the properties of a substance, I will also clear the ground from possible objections to it based on Aristotle's language in *Metaphysics* Z.3. I acknowledge that his words may at times be (unintentionally) misleading.

---

[65] Aristotle's language is misleadingly suggestive of a particular entity, here, as he uses the term τί (something) in describing the ἔσχατον ὑποκείμενον (ultimate subject).

[66] I am not convinced by Aristotle that Plato thought that space is the partaker that is qualified by the copies of the Forms that enter the Receptacle. However, I will not argue for this here.

[67] This is not a negation of my position in Marmodoro (2022b), but rather a deeper understanding of what I call there the function of subjecthood.

My general position is that when and where Aristotle's language might be less straightforward than we would want, we need to bear in mind that he is innovating metaphysically, without having the appropriate terminology yet. Innovating metaphysically is one thing; but innovating the terminology that describes the metaphysical innovation is quite another.

My understanding of the role of ultimate of matter in *Metaphysics* Z.3 and my claim that some of the statements that Aristotle makes are misleading (rather than ground for objecting to my interpretation) are based on what Aristotle does *not* do, although we would have expected him to have done. Let me give an example. Aristotle's most misleading statement in *Metaphysics* Z.3 is the following: 'the predicates other than substance are predicated of substance, while substance [along with all the properties predicated of it] is predicated of matter' (1029a23). I understand it as saying: the predicates (other than the substantial form) are *predicated of* the substantial form as subject, while the substantial form *occurs* in matter. On first reading, Aristotle's s sentence negates my interpretation, by explicitly saying that there are *two subjects* of properties in every substance, where matter is the subject of the substantial form and all the other properties of the subsance. However, this would be metaphysically unacceptable for Aristotle, contradicting the most fundamental theses of his metaphysics, from the *Categories* onwards. *If* Aristotle were committed to the view that there are two different subjects in each substance, and that the essence of a substance is predicated of its matter, it would be unthinkable – or at the very least *very* surprising – that he would never come back and consider the implications of this position; but he does not, ever. His stance is consistently that there is only one subject in a substance, its instantiated substantial form, which is one, which unifies the components of the substance, and which is what the substance is in itself (*kath' hauto*). Aristotle's language misleads us into thinking that matter is reified as a subject of properties simply because he had not developed yet the terminology that would enable him or anyone else to describe everything that he is doing in his metaphysical system.

To bring together the numerous theses argued for in Sections 4.2 and 4.3, I have argued that Aristotle views the instantiation of a property as a complex metaphysical process, by which a property becomes a qualification of a subject (Section 4.2). The mere presence of a property in a subject (substance) does not entail that the property qualifies the substance – a difference that Plato explicitly identified in the *Lysis* (217d, as we saw in Section 2.4), but which the Bundle Theories of all times, from Anaxagoras onwards, do not not acknowledge or cannot explain metaphysically. A discrete property in a substance would be a *part* of the substance and would not qualify the substance (as Plato makes clear in the passage from the *Lysis* quoted in Section 2.4).

Aristotle sees the difference between the presence of a property and its being a qualification of the substance as a question of what would make the property belong to the substance, so that the property characterises the substance. For Aristotle, it is all about the discreteness of the substance *versus* the discreteness of its property components. For Aristotle there is only one operative criterion of individuation in a substance: that of the substantial form. So in Socrates, every property that is intantiated in him qualifies the form of 'human being' in him. This, I argue, is what it is for a property to be *instantiated* in a substance, for Aristotle, to *qualify* the substance. Of course, for essences, namely for substantial forms, instantiation is metaphysically the reverse – they provide the individuation criterion for other properties which thereby qualify the substances. So essences, namley substantial forms, are *instantiated*, for Aristotle, by *becoming qualified* by properties.

I have further argued that in *Metaphysic* Z.3, Aristotle is not describing the metaphysical phenomenon of instantiation, namely of a property becoming the qualification of a substance. I contend that he is there describing a closely related phenomenon, for which there is no specific term, namely when a property becomes *actual, occurring* in nature. If a property qualifies an entity, it does not follow that the property is in nature, for example if the propery qualifies an entity that is an abstract universal – for example if being 'rational' qualifies the universal 'human'. So, while if a property *occurs* in nature, it qualifies (a thing in nature, for example Socrates as a rational person); if a property *qualifies* (a thing, for example the universal 'human'), it does not follow that it occurs in nature.

I have further addressed whether the ultimate matter Aristotle introduces in *Metaphysics* Z.3 is the subject which is qualified by the properties that occur in it (which Aristotle's language misleadingly seems to suggest). I have shown that this is not and could not be the case, on the basis of what Aristotle says about it. The reason is that ultimate matter, which, as Aristotle tells us, is devoid of particularity and devoid of any properties and generally categorial being, has no individuation criterion to offer to the properties that would (hypothetically) qualify it. Aristotle says explicitly that ultimate matter is not an individual (not a τόδε τι, 1029a28). So, it is clear that the properties that *occur in the ultimate matter* do not and cannot qualify it as their subject: rather, that they are 'en-mattered' signifies here that the properties come to be present in nature, *occurring* as *actual* properties in nature.

4.4 The *Essence Regress*

We saw, when examining Plato's theory, that the division of an entity into parts is not the only type of division that threatens the oneness of an entity. There is a second type of division, into *subject and essence*. Plato posited Forms to be what they are *in themselves* (*kath' hauta*); he wanted identity, rather than metaphysical division between a Form and its essence. Nevertheless, Plato did (*per hypothesis*) split a Form and its essence in the TBA, when he talked of the form of a Form. The form of a Form is (using Aristotelian terminology) the essence of a Form predicated of (and metaphysically divided from) the Form as its subject. The TMA Regress on the other hand ensues from the explicitly posited division between the essence of each Form and the Form, *ad infinitum*. I argued (in Section 3.4) that Plato solved this problem by *fiat*, in the *Timaeus*, where the *paradeigma* is what it is without ever having become what it is. I argued that *predication is a type of becoming*: the essence of a Form *makes* the Form what it is. Plato rejected becoming in the World of Being in the *Timaeus*, and so rejected essential predication in the World of the *paradeigma*, thereby blocking the TMA Regress. I argue here that Aristotle faces the same problem in *Metaphysics* Z.6. The problem at its core is whether the essence of a substance brings to the substance 'something' that the substance does not have on its own, thereby making it what it is. In the context of the TBA, the subject is the Form (F_3), which is unique, and the essence if its form (f_3) which, as we have seen, recurs, as a universal, in F_1, F_2 and F_3. In Plato, this division is not overcome, because nothing in Plato's ontology unifies a particular and a universal. Aristotle takes this problem very seriously and analyses it into two types of problems, with two different solutions. One is the Platonic type of division *of a form* into subject and essence, for example the property of 'being white' is essentially white. The second type of division is that *of a physical substance* into subject and essence. On my understanding, Aristotle treats the first type of division as a semantic (logical/conceptual) division, and only the second type as ontological – I will show that he argued accordingly. Here we will address only the first type of division. Aristotle writes:

> The absurdity of the separation [subject-essence] would appear also if one were to assign a name to each of the essences; for there would be another essence besides the original one, e.g. to the essence of horse will belong a second essence. (1031b27-30)

Aristotle puts an abrupt end to this division, and to the ensuing regress, thus: 'Yet why should not some things be their essence from the start?' (1031b31). Implicit reply: there is no reason why not. Let me generalise this result: Aristotle has in mind essences (substantial forms) such as being human; he proposes that the essence 'what it is to be a human being is' does not divide into subject–essence, and is therefore 'just' the essence (εὐθὺς τί ἦν εἶναι) of what it is to be a human being. So, for Aristotle, essences do not divide into subject and essence. This is also what I take Plato's solution from the *Timaeus* to be: it blocks becoming in the realm of Being, and so, on my reading, blocks essential predications of Forms.

I take Aristotle to feel free to block the regress in this way, because he sees the subject–essence division in an essence as logical/conceptual. He accordingly holds there is no ontological division between subject and essence. Thinking retrospectively, in the light of Aristotle's *Essence Regress*, we can with hindsight read the subject–essence division in the TBA, between the Form (F_3) and the form (f_3) of a Form, also to be semantic rather than ontological. (This would have saved the *kath' hauto* nature of Platonic Forms.) By contrast, the division between a person and her essence is ontological in Aristotle's metaphysical system. This division first emerges in the *Categories*, and it is ultimately resolved in *Metaphysics* Z.17, as we will see.

4.5 Physical Matter

Before coming to the analysis of Aristotle's argument in *Metaphysics* Z.17 (here in Section 4.6), I want first to quote a short passage in which he explicitly states the oneness of a physical substance. He says that the definition of a substance must be one in so far as it is the definition of a substance, which is one:

> But surely all the attributes in the definition *must* be one; for the definition is a single formula and a formula of substance, so that *it must be* a formula of some *one thing*; *for substance means a 'one' and a 'this'*, as we maintain. (1037b24-27, my emphasis)[68]

What type of oneness is Aristotle referring to here? We saw in Section 4.1 that for Aristotle in the *Categories* a substance consists of a substantial form (namely its essence), and its non-substantial properties. I showed that Aristotle states there that the properties that make up a substance are not parts of it. So, for Aristotle in the *Categories*, for example Socrates consists of the substantial form 'human being', which is qualified by all the properties of Socrates that are 'in' him, not as parts, but in a partless whole; as such, it is unified into one (*à la* Plato's account of unified partless wholes in the *Theaetetus*).

I want further to claim that, in the *Categories*, the qualified essence of a physical substance, for example Socrates, is not only unified as a *type* of substance by its essence, but that it is also a *particular*, in virtue of its qualifications. I argue that for Aristotle, particularity is *not* grounded on matter. My first argument is that Aristotle is explicit about the numerical oneness of physical

---

[68] In the original: δεῖ δέ γε ἓν [εἶναι ὅσα ἐν τῷ ὁρισμῷ· ὁ γὰρ ὁρισμὸς λόγος τίς ἐστιν εἷς καὶ οὐσίας, ὥστε ἑνός τινος δεῖ αὐτὸν εἶναι λόγον· καὶ γὰρ ἡ οὐσία ἕν τι καὶ τόδε τι σημαίνει, ὡς φαμέν.

substances in the *Categories*, where matter is not part of his ontology; and its absence does not leave an explanatory lacuna. He writes:

> It seems most distinctive of substance that what is *numerically one* [ἓν ἀριθμῷ] and the same is able to receive contraries. In no other case could one bring forward anything, *numerically one* [ἓν ἀριθμῷ], which is able to receive contraries. For example, a colour which is *numerically one* [ἀριθμῷ] and the same will not be black and white, nor will *numerically one* [ἀριθμῷ] and the same action be bad and good; and similarly with everything else that is not substance. A substance, however, *numerically one* and the same [οὐσία ἓν καὶ ταὐτὸν ἀριθμῷ ὄν], is able to receive contraries. For example, an *individual man* – one and the same – becomes pale at one time and dark at another, and hot and cold, and bad and good. (4a10 ff, my emphasis)

Aristotle is an empiricist, and so for him the qualitative difference between substances would be sufficient for their numerical difference. (See Section 4.3 for qualifications of this principle.) So, the *Categories'* ontology suffices for grounding the particularity of physical substances, and accordingly, Aristotle talks in the *Categories* of substances as being numerically one.

I further argue that the reason matter does not enter the picture in the *Categories* is not because Aristotle had not thought about matter yet, before the *Physics*, but because he did not need matter in the *Categories'* ontology of numerically one physical substances. We have evidence that Aristotle had a clear conception of underlying matter receiving properties, from Plato's conception of the Receptacle in the *Timaeus*.

Finally, matter does answer a metaphysical problem in Aristotle's *Physics*, which does not arise in the *Categories*, and which does not require any addition to the ontology of the *Categories*. Matter is needed only to answer the Parmenidean strictures on existence and coming-to-be, which Aristotle addresses in his *Physics* I.8. Briefly, when a new substance is generated, a particular quantity of matter of the old substance survives, and receives the new form. So, for example, a quantity of marble, of a marble cube, survives as it is shaped into a statue; the marble that survives is common between the cube and the statue. The quantity of matter is particular, that is numerically one, in virtue of the properties that qualify it and single it out among other things in the world. Nothing more than the ontology of the *Categories* is needed to establish the numerical oneness of the matter that survives a transformation. By that I mean that for Aristotle a substance is only its properties, unified, namely only the items in the categorial scheme that qualify the substance and constitute it.[69]

---

[69] A substance is constituted by a substantial form (i.e. its species form) qualified by its non-substantial properties (in the categorial scheme). The bodily matter of the substance is consituted by properties, too. See also footnote 77, and Marmodoro (2018) for the supporting arguments.

He does not need more ontology to account for the metaphysics of substances, except for the account of how properties occur in the world, which he gives in *Metaphysics* Z.3; but even this does not add any categorial beings to the ontology of a substance.

To conclude, the advantage of the *Categories'* ontology sufficing for the numerical oneness (i.e. particularity) of a substance is that numerical oneness derives from the essence of the substance, as is qualified by its properties. I want to emphasise the difference between this account and Plato's TBA, where the subject (F_3) is particular and the essence (f_3) is universal. In the TBA, the subject and its essence are different entities: the one particular and the other universal. In Aristotle's *Categories* ontology, the subject and the essence are, by contrast, the same entity; the substance is the qualified essence. This is the import of Aristotle's saying in the *Categories* that the definition of the substantial form (the essence) is predicated of the substance (2a19 ff.), but not the definition of the substance's other properties (2a29-34); so 'what a substance is'[70] is given by the definition of its essence, which is the only definition that is true of the substance.

4.6 The *Syllable Argument*

As I understand Aristotle's metaphysical system, he drafts an ontological position on substances in the *Categories*, and concludes with the same position in *Metaphysics* Z.17, having developed more sophisticated explanations for the claims and assumptions made initially in the *Categories*. The position was first introduced in Plato's *Theaetetus*, but built on ambiguities and unexplained metaphysical assumptions, which are gradually identified and addressed by Aristotle, and developed into metaphysical positions that explain and justify them (primarily) in Book Z of the *Metaphysics*. I submit that *Metaphysics* Z.17 is the culmination and development of Plato's position in the *Theaetetus*, which we encountered already in Aristotle's *Categories*. The common position that goes through all these texts and arguments is that a substance is not reducible to its components; rather, a substance is complex, made from different components, but is one, unified by a form.[71] What changes, I argue, from the *Theaetetus* to *Metaphysics* Z.17 is that whereas the components in the

---

[70] The truly predicated definition of the substantial form brings with it the individuation criterion by which the substance is individuated, for example as a man.

[71] Thus, in *Metaphysics* Z.17, Aristotle argues:

'Now since that which is composed of something in such a way that the whole is a unity; not as an aggregate is a unity, but as a syllable is – the syllable is not the letters, nor is BA the same as B and A; nor is flesh fire and earth; because after dissolution the compounds, e.g. flesh or the syllable, no longer exist; but the letters exist, and so do fire and earth' (1041b10-15).

Theaetetus are types, for example 'S' and 'O' of syllable 'SO', the components in the *Syllable Argument* of Z.17 are elements, namely instantiated physical particulars (e.g. flesh, made of fire and earth 1041b1-15; also, as Aristotle explains: 'An *element* is that which is present as matter in a thing, and into which the thing is divided; for example, *a* and *b* are the elements of the syllable' 1041b31-2). Moving from the unification of types to the unification of particular physical components in a substance is a game changer. Whereas unifying types results in qualitative uniformity, unifying *instantiated* types (elements) results in the particularity (uniqueness) of the substance. In *Metaphysics* Z.17, Aristotle establishes that the Platonic position in the *Theaetetus* – that a form unifies the component types of a complex thing into one type, of the form – extends also to the unification of the instantiated components of a complex into a substance. I take Aristotle to be claiming that the unification solution remains the same in kind, even when what is unified are instantiated types or properties; for example, syllable 'SO' is unified by its form into one, whether its components are types, 'S' and 'O', or its components are instantiated types, for example the written letters 'S' and 'O'. The reason must be that the instantiation of a type does not undermine the unification of the types (in a substance) by the form. We saw in *Metaphysics* Z.3 that according to Aristotle the instantiation of a property does not add more ontology or categorial being to it, and so, we should not expect that the instantiation of properties should interfere with their unification by the substance's form.

In *Metaphysics* Z.17, Aristotle develops an argument, which I have elsewhere referred to as the *Syllable Argument*,[72] and which aims to show that a substance is unified into one by its substantial form. I reproduce here the text for ease of reference for the reader:

> As regards that which is compounded out of something so that the whole is one – not like a heap, however, but like a syllable – the syllable is not its elements, *ba* is not the same as *b* and *a*, nor is flesh fire and earth; for when they are dissolved the wholes, i.e. the flesh and the syllable, no longer exist, but the elements of the syllable exist, and so do fire and earth. The syllable, then, is something – not only its elements (the vowel and the consonant) but also something else; and the flesh is not only fire and earth or the hot and the cold, but also something else. Since then that something must be either an element or composed of elements, if it is an element the same argument will again apply; for flesh will consist of this and fire and earth and something still further, so that the process will go on to infinity; while if it is a compound clearly it will be a compound not of one but of many (or else it will itself be that one), so that again in this case we can use the same argument as in the

---

[72] I have advanced in my understanding of this text since Marmodoro (2013).

case of flesh or of the syllable. But it would seem that this is something, and
not an element, and that it is the cause which makes *this* thing flesh and *that*
a syllable. And similarly in all other cases. And ths is the substance of each
thing: for this is the primary cause of its being; . . . their substance would seem
to be this nature which is not an element but a principle. (1041b11-28)

Here Aristotle argues that what unifies the elements that make something one
cannot be a further element, on pain of regress, but has to be something else,
which for Aristotle is the substantial form (see the lines 1041b25-29). This is
also a vindication of Plato's claim in the *Theaetetus*, or more precisely, an
explanation that a complex of components, for example syllable 'SO', is unified
by a *form*, not by a further component of the whole. We encounter the position
again in the *Categories*, where the properties 'in' the substance are not parts of
it, so the whole is unified into a partless one. The position is further developed
into a metaphysical account of qualification, in *Metaphysics Z*, where the
properties 'in' the substantial form are not compresent with the form, but now
qualify the form, thereby establishing the qualitative unity (uniformity) of the
substance. The same position is finally shown in *Metaphysics Z*.17 to establish
that the qualitative unity of the substance is also numerical unity. The reason is
not stated by Aristotle, but it is derived from his metaphysical theory, namely
that the properties 'in' the substantial form (as in the *Categories*) qualify the
form (as in *Metaphysics Z*.1), and so instantiate it and particularise it;[73] therefore, the *qualitative* unity (uniformity) of a substance resulting from the qualification of its form is also a *numerical* unity.[74] This is what Aristotle tells us in
Metaphysics Z.17; the 'elements' referred to there are nothing but the instantiated properties in the substance,[75] namely when inter-qualification has taken
place between the properties, rather than mere compresence. So, Aristotle is
claiming in *Metaphysics Z*.17 that the form of a complex, for example of
a substance, not only unify the properties of the substance into a partless
whole (as Aristotle claims in the *Categories*), but it also unifies these properties
as instantiated (as particular elements) in the substance.

In conclusion, *instantiation is qualification*, and not some inexplicable primitive way of gaining particularity; qualification is sufficient for the *particularity*
of the substance.

---

[73] It is the substance, namely the substantial form as qualified by the properties, that is particular,
namely unique in its ontological context; and the substance's matter, too, derives its numerical
particularity from the qualified form – the substance. Traditionally, the reverse is thought to be
Aristotle's position – the particularity of substance derives from the particularity of its matter.

[74] Which is what allows Aristotle to talk of numerical oneness in the *Categories*, as we saw in
Section 4.5.

[75] For fire and earth are metaphysically reducible to the properties that make them up. I argued for
this in Marmodoro (2018).

4.7 Particularity

Aristotle develops a general metaphysical approach to the problem of the unity of substances which is genuinely revolutionary. In a word, a substance is unified into one by its form – qualitatively as well as numerically. Within Aristotle's metaphysical system, the top-down oneness of a substance, as unified by its form, 'trickles down' to the numerical unity of its elements. That qualitative oneness determined numerical oneness too, in a substance, in Aristotle, is verified also by his metaphysical doctrine of the *Homonymy Principle*. In the *Metaphysics*, the principle is stated thus:

> [The parts of a substance] cannot even exist if severed from the whole; for it is not a finger in any state that is the finger of a living thing, but the dead finger is a finger only homonymously. (1035b24-25)

The thrust of the principle is that a part of a substance is what it is on account of the substance's substantial form. It is individuated differently as a part of the substance rather than as severed from the substance (e.g. a severed finger is not a finger, but is a-finger-only-in-name). That is, the numerically single/particular elements of a substance exist only in the substance, because even their numerical identity has been determined by the substantial form of the substance. For example, an animal is constituted of material parts that are what they are in virtue of the form of the animal.

So, the metaphysical challenge that Aristotle addresses is this: can one account for the oneness and uniqueness of a substance by means of the substance being the qualified substantial form 'all the way down'? No philosopher before Aristotle achieves this, but Aristotle does, by deriving numerical particularity (uniqueness) from the qualitative oneness (uniformity) of a substance, in his empiricist metaphysics.[76] So Aristotle does not need to divide a substance into matter and form, hylomorphically, to render it particular.[77] I argued in Section 4.2 that Aristotle employs two metaphysical mechanisms for the unification of properties of a substance as its qualifications: first, *eliminating* the individuality of the property that is predicated of a substance; and second, *embedding* the individuality of the substance in the properties predicated of it. We can now see that in effect both these mechanisms are metaphysical

---

[76] That is, the qualifications of a substance suffice in rendering it unique, particular, for empiricist intents and purposes.

[77] By 'hylomorphic' here I mean the division of a substance into matter and essence, where matter is supposed to confer particularity to the essence. This is not the bodily matter, which serves different purposes in Aristotle's metaphysics, and which derives its particularity from the particularity of its substance.

implementations of the *Homonymy Principle*, showing how/why a substance is its qualified essential form 'all the way down' – delivering particularity.

4.8 Conclusion

Aristotle was a student of Plato, and never stopped learning from him. I have tried to outline here Aristotle's metaphysical development towards understanding the role that properties play in a substance, especially the metaphysical role of the essence (the substantial form) of a substance. As I understand him, Aristotle started with a Platonic position on the ontology of substances, with regard to the role of the substantial form in unifying the properties of a substance, and developed it further, with explanations and justifications within his own metaphysical system. I argued that for Aristotle in the *Categories* a substance is qualified by the properties it unifies into a whole (that has no parts). Aristotle develops in the *Metaphysics* a much more sophisticated account than Plato of how the form unifies partlessly the property components of a substance. At the same time, Aristotle's account of qualification explains how properties are instantiated, in substances.

This is how Aristotle establishes that each substance is *kath' hauto f*. In retrospect, when Plato says in the TBA that a Form (F_3) has a form (f_3), expressing that a Form has an essential nature, one is at a loss as to what the Form (F_3) might be, since it is divided from its essence. All one can say there is that the subject is particular, and the essence universal. This is a problem: the subject–essence division is the greatest threat for the oneness of a substance. I claim Aristotle resolved this problem through his *Embedding Principle*, which explains the qualification of a substance, the instantiation of its properties and the particularity of the substance. So, a substance is *kath' hauto* its essence, where the substance is identical to its qualified essence. The substance is the essence qualified by the substance's properties, by means of the *Embedding Principle*. For instance, the human being is wise. If particularity were primitive, for example due to prime matter, the division between subject and essence would be unbridgeable; while for Aristotle, particularity is grounded on qualification, and qualities are unified by the form.

5 Conclusion

It is widely held among metaphysicians that properties are reified to explain what it is for objects to be qualified and similar to one another. What type of entity should a property be to explain qualification and similarity? I have here examined the views of Anaxagoras, Plato and Aristotle, and argued that they devised different models, each one more profound and explanatorily powerful than its predecessor. Anaxagoras reifies properties, which are physical entities in nature, for example the Opposite property Hot. Thereby, qualification and similarity are explained according to a version of the *Distributive Model*, where the parts of a property F (e.g. the Opposite Hot) are distributed among many different objects qualifying them as f (e.g. as hot). This is an early model because it works by, so to speak, 'cloning' the source of *f-ness* through its parts; a thing is hot if it has parts of the Hot in it (in preponderance). Such an account cannot but fail as a full explanation of qualification and similarity because it presupposes them; the account cannot explain why the parts of a source of *f-ness* are *f*, for example hot, and similar between them with respect to *f-ness*, both of which are primitively assumed in the theory.

Plato, too, adopted for the most part of thinking the *Distributive Model*, and held that properties, his Forms, are distributed to objects by each object partaking of a part of a Form. Thus partaking of Form F qualifies the object as an *f*, and if both *a* and *b* partake of Form F, they are similar to one another. Plato himself discovered in the TMA that the *Distributive Model* divides ontologically a qualification from what it qualifies – a problem that Aristotle solved in his theory of substance. Plato eventually criticises and abandons the *Distributive Model* of explanation; however, I argued that he also takes the first steps towards the discovery of recurring universals in the TBA. The *Recurrence Model* of explanation that emerges from Plato's texts is altogether different from the *Distributive Model*, by explaining qualification and similarity through a single entity that recurs whole in the different similars, rather than through different entities that are themselves similar, deriving from the same source.

Aristotle champions the conception of properties as recurring universals, thereby offering a novel account of qualification and similarity in terms of recurrence. Aristotle's solution is sometimes viewed with suspicion, because he does not explain explicitly how recurrence works. However, I suggested that recurrence in Aristotle is to be understood in terms of abstraction. A universal property recurs in similar objects if we can abstract this property away from each of these objects. Abstraction is the metaphysical converse of the instantiation of a property in a substance. As the converse of instantiation, abstraction too is metaphysically complex, and still awaiting more analysis.

What I tried to show in this Element is that although qualification and similarity are driving forces shaping our conception of properties as particulars or as universals, there are kindred metaphysical problems which preoccupied the ancient philosophers we examined and which affected their conceptions of the role that properties have in the constitution of objects.

Overall, I have endeavoured to make attractive Aristotle's conception of properties as recurrent universals, even for our own contemporary metaphysical concerns. I addressed the challenging topic of the instantiation of universals in substances, through qualification, and how they relate to particularity. This was a key breakthrough in Aristotelian metaphysics, because it makes it possible to derive the particularity of substances from a combination of non-particular qualities, thereby avoiding an unbridgeable division in a substance between two kinds of oneness, namely particularity and qualitiative uniformity.

In concluding, I want to emphasise that there is much metaphysics, explicit or not, still to be worked out and understood in ancient philosophical texts. More specifically, there is more to learn from the ancients in the domain of the metaphysics of properties. That much is still left for us to learn is partly due to the fact that the ancients are not as descriptive of what they were proposing in their metaphysics as later philosophers would have wanted them to be. Partly, I argue, we too need to be open to venture into their proposals, even when not fully described by them.

References

Translations of the Primary Texts

Barnes, J. (ed.) (1984), *The Complete Works of Aristotle*, 2 vols. The Revised Oxford Translation – Bollingen Series.

Cooper, J. M. (ed.) (1997), *Plato: Complete Works*, Hackett.

Curd, P. (2007), *Anaxagoras of Clazomenae*. Fragments and Testimonia. A text and translation with notes and essays by Patricia Curd. University of Toronto Press.

Secondary Literature

Ackrill, J. L. (1963), Aristotle *Categories* and *De Interpretatione*, Clarendon University Press.

Allen, S. (2016), *A Critical Introduction to Properties*, Bloomsbury.

Armstrong D. M. (1978), *Nominalism and Realism*, Cambridge University Press.

(1989), *A Combinatorial Theory of Possibility*, Cambridge University Press.

(1980), 'Against "Ostrich" Nominalism: A Reply to Michael Devitt', *Pacific Philosophical Quarterly* 61(4): 440–9.

Bäck, A. (2014), *Aristotle's Theory of Abstraction*, Springer.

Black, M. (1952), 'The Identity of Indiscernibles', *Mind, New Series* 61(242): 153–64.

Brentlinger, J. (1972), 'Incomplete Predicates and the Two-World Theory of the *Phaedo*', *Phronesis* 17(1): 61–79.

Burnyear, M. (2001), *A Map of Metaphysics Zeta*, Mathesis.

Campbell, K. (1990), *Abstract Particulars*, Basil Blackwell.

Chiaradonna, R. and Galluzzo, G. (eds.) (2013), *Universals in Ancient Philosophy*, Edizioni della Normale, 113–37.

Cohen, S. M. (1999), 'The Logic of the Third Man', *The Philosophical Review* 80(4): 448–75.

Costa, D. (2019), 'An Argument against Aristotelian Universals', *Synthese* 198: 4331–8.

Della Rocca, M. (2020), *The Parmenidean Ascent*, Oxford University Press.

Denyer, N. (1983), 'Plato's Theory of Stuffs', *Philosophy* 58: 315–27.

Fine, K. (1998), *The Limits of Abstraction*, Oxford University Press.

Fine, G. (1983), 'Plato and Aristotle on Form and Substance', *Proceedings of the Cambridge Philological Society, New Series* 29 (209): 23–47.

(1993), *On Ideas: Aristotle's Criticism of Plato's Theory of Forms*, Clarendon Press.

(2008), *The Oxford Handbook on Plato*, Oxford University Press.

Frey, C. (2015), 'From Blood to Flesh: Homonymy, Unity, and Ways of Being in Aristotle', *Ancient Philosophy* 35 (2): 375–94.

Galluzzo, G. and Loux, M. J. (eds.) (2015), *The Problem of Universals in Contemporary Philosophy*, Cambridge University Press.

Gill, M.-L. (1989), *Aristotle on Substance: The Paradox of Unity*, Princeton University Press.

González-Varela, J. E. (2020), 'The One over Many Principle of *Republic* 596a', *Apeiron* 53 (4): 339–61.

Harte, V. (2002), *Plato on Parts and Wholes: The Metaphysics of Structure*, Oxford University Press.

(2008), 'Plato's Metaphysics', in Fine, G. (ed.), *The Oxford Handbook of Plato*, Oxford University Press, 455–80.

(2009), 'What's a Particular, and What Makes It So? Some Thoughts, Mainly about Aristotle', in Sharples, R. (ed.), *Particulars in Greek Philosophy*, Brill, 97–125.

Jaworski, W. (2016), *Structure and the Metaphysics of Mind*. Oxford University Press.

Koons, R. (2014), 'Staunch vs. Faint-Hearted Hylomorphism: Toward an Aristotelian Account of Composition', *Res Philosophica* 91: 1–27.

Koslicki, K. (2008), *The Structure of Objects*, Oxford University Press.

(2018), *Form, Matter, Substance*, Oxford University Press.

Krizan, M. (2016), 'Prime Matter without Extension', *Journal of the History of Philosophy* 54 (4): 523–46.

(2018), 'Primary Qualities and Aristotle's Elements', *Ancient Philosophy* 38 (1): 91–112.

Lewis, D. (1983), 'New Work for a Theory of Universals', *Australasian Journal of Philosophy* 61(4):343–77.

(1986), *On the Plurality of Worlds*, Blackwell.

(1991), *Parts of Classes*, Wiley-Blackwell.

Loux, M. (1991), *Primary Ousia: An Essay on Aristotle's Metaphysics Z and H*, Cornell University Press.

Lowe, E. J. (2006), *The Four-Category Ontology*, Oxford University Press.

(2012), 'A Neo-Aristotelian Substance Ontology: Neither Relational Nor Constituent', in Tahko, T. (ed.), *Contemporary Aristotelian Metaphysics*, Cambridge University Press, 229–48.

Mann, W. R. (2000), *The Discovery of Things: Aristotle's* Categories *and Their Context*, Princeton University Press.

Mann W-R., (2000), *The Discovery of Things: Aristotle's Categories and Their Context*. Princeton University Press.

Marmodoro, A. (2008), "'Is *Being One* Only One?" – The Argument for the Uniqueness of Platonic Forms', *Apeiron*XLI (4), 211–27.

(2013), 'Aristotle's Hylomorphism without Reconditioning', *Philosophical Inquiry* 37(1/2): 5–22.

(2015), 'Anaxagoras's Qualitative Gunk', *British Journal for the History of Philosophy* 23(3): 402–22.

(2017), *Everything in Everything*: *Anaxagoras's Metaphysics*, Oxford University Press.

(2018), 'Potentiality in Aristotle's Metaphysics', in Engelhard, K. and Quante, M. (eds.), *The Handbook of Potentiality*, Springer, 15–43.

(2020), 'Hylomorphic Unity', in Bliss, R. and Miller, R. (eds.), *The Routledge Handbook of Metametaphysics*, 284–99.

(2021), *Forms and Structure in Plato's Metaphysics*, Oxford University Press.

(2022a), 'Instantiation', *Metaphysics* 4(1): 32–46.

(2022b), 'Why Studying the History of Philosophy Matters', *Think. A Journal of the Royal Institute for Philosophy* 21(60): 5–20.

Maurin, A.-S. (2018), 'Tropes', in Zalta, E. N. (ed.), *Stanford Encyclopedia of Philosophy*. https://plato.stanford.edu/archives/sum2018/entries/tropes.

(2022), *Properties*, Cambridge University Press.

McCabe, M. M. (1999). *Plato's Individuals*, Princeton.

Moore, G. E. (1925), 'A Defense of Common Sense', in Muirhead, J. H. (ed.), *Contemporary British Philosophy*, George Allen and Unwin, 192–233.

Orilia, F. and Paolini Paoletti, M. (2020) 'Properties', in Zalta, E. N. (ed.), *Stanford Encyclopedia of Philosophy*. https://plato.stanford.edu/entries/properties/.

Parry, R. D. (1980), 'The Uniqueness Proof for Forms in *Republic* 10', *Journal of the History of Philosophy* 23.

Peterson Siebels, A. (2018), 'Unity and Plurality in Hylomorphic Composition', *Australasian Journal of Philosophy* 96 (1): 1–13.

Ramsey, F. P. (1925), 'Universals', *Mind* 34: 401–17.

Rodriguez-Pereyra, G. (2000), 'What Is the Problem of Universals?', *Mind* 109 (434): 255–73.

(2019) 'Nominalism in Metaphysics', in Zalta, E. N. (ed.), *Stanford Encyclopedia of Philosophy*. https://plato.stanford.edu/entries/nominalism-metaphysics/. https://plato.stanford.edu/archives/sum2019/entries/nominalism-metaphysics.

Scaltsas, T. (1990), 'Is a Whole Identical to Its Parts?', *Mind* XCIX (396): 583–99.

(1994), *Substances and Universals in Aristotle's Metaphysics*, Cornell University Press.

Schofield, M. (1972), '*Metaph. Z* 3: Some Suggestions', *Phronesis* 17 (2): 97–101.

(1980), *An Essay on Anaxagoras*, Cambridge University Press.

Schofield, M. (1996), 'Likeness and Likenesses in the Parmenides', in Christopher Gill and Mary Margaret McCabe (eds.), *Form and Argument in Late Plato*, Oxford University Press, 49–77.

Sedley, D. (2013), 'Plato and the One-Over-Many Principle' in Chiaradonna, R. and Galluzzo, G. (eds.), *Universals in Ancient Philosophy*, Edizioni della Normale, 113–37.

Shields, C. (2022), 'Hylomorphisms', *Dialogoi. Ancient Philosophy Today* 4 (1): 96–127.

Sider, T. (1995), 'Sparseness, Immanence, and Naturalness', *Noûs* 29: 360–77.

Simpson, W. (2023), *Hylomorphism*, Cambridge University Press.

Silverman, A. (2002), *The Dialectic of Essence: A Study of Plato's Metaphysics*, Princeton University Press.

Strang, C. (1972), 'Plato and the Third Man', in Vlastos, G. (ed.), *Plato: Metaphysics and Epistemolgy Vol. I*. Macmillan, 184–200.

Vlastos, G. (1950), 'The physical theory of Anaxagoras', *The Philosophical Review* 59 (1): 31–57.

Vlastos, G. (1965), 'The "Third Man" Argument in the *Parmenides*', in Allen, R. E. (ed.), *Studies in Plato's Metaphysics*, Routledge and Kegan, 231–63.

(1969), 'Plato's "Third Man" Argument (*Parm.* 132a1-b2): Text and Logic', *Philosophical Quarterly* 19: 289–381.

Wedin, M. V. (2000), *Aristotle's Theory of Substance. The* Categories *and* Metaphysics Z. Oxford University Press.

Acknowledgements

My thanks are due in the first place to the series editor, James Warren, and the anonymous readers, for the two rounds of constructive feedback they provided on the manuscript. Earlier versions of the manuscript were presented and discussed at the Universidad Nacional Autónoma de México (in 2022), and at the Universities of Notre Dame and Purdue in the United States (in 2023), where colleagues and students offered many helpful comments; I am grateful to all of them, and to the History of Philosophy Forum which sponsored my research stay at Notre Dame. Two further institutions supported the initial and final phases of the work, respectively: the *Wissenschaftkollege zü Berlin* in Germany (2021–2) and the *Fondation Maison Des Sciences de l'Homme* in France (2023).

Cambridge Elements ⹇

Ancient Philosophy

James Warren

University of Cambridge

James Warren is Professor of Ancient Philosophy at the University of Cambridge. He is the author of *Epicurus and Democritean Ethics* (Cambridge, 2002), *Facing Death: Epicurus and his Critics* (2004), *Presocratics* (2007) and *The Pleasures of Reason in Plato, Aristotle and the Hellenistic Hedonists* (Cambridge, 2014). He is also the editor of *The Cambridge Companion to Epicurus* (Cambridge, 2009), and joint editor of *Authors and Authorities in Ancient Philosophy* (Cambridge, 2018).

About the Series

The Elements in Ancient Philosophy series deals with a wide variety of topics and texts in ancient Greek and Roman philosophy, written by leading scholars in the field. Taking a theme, question, or type of argument, some Elements explore it across antiquity and beyond. Others look in detail at an ancient author, a specific work, or a part of a longer work, considering its structure, content, and significance, or explore more directly ancient perspectives on modern philosophical questions.

Cambridge Elements ≡

Ancient Philosophy